Who is This?

Who is This?

Holy Week Meditations and Other Sermons 1998–2000

Eric James

MOWBRAY
London and New York

IN MEMORIAM
and with admiration, affection and gratitude
Robert Runcie
Archbishop of Canterbury

Mowbray
A Continuum imprint
The Tower Building, 11 York Road, London SE1 7NX
370 Lexington Avenue, New York NY 10017-6503

First published 2001

British Library Cataloguing-in-Publication Data
A catalogue record for this book is available from the British Library.

ISBN 0-264-67533-9

Typeset by BookEns Ltd, Royston, Herts
Printed and bound in Great Britain by Biddles Ltd,
Guildford and King's Lynn

Contents

CONTENTS

Preface

It was a particular pleasure to return in 1999, the last year of the old millennium, to St Stephen's, Rochester Row, Westminster – where I served as a curate 50 years ago – to preach on Palm Sunday, on each evening in Holy Week, during the Good Friday service and on Easter Day. I am thankful that my publishers now want to make the addresses I gave then form the first part of this sixth book of sermons I have had published, and to make the whole book their Lent Book for 2002.

It seems to me now, after 50 years of ministry, that the question 'Who is This?' remains the very heart of preaching.

I am greatly honoured that the retired Archbishop of Canterbury, Robert Runcie, allowed me to dedicate this volume to him. It was sad that, having said he would like to write a Foreword for it, his death prevented him from doing so. But that loss is small compared with the loss his death has been to his family and to so many of his friends. I take hope and comfort from that marvellous prayer in the 1980 Alternative Service Book, which has been carried on into the new Common Worship:

> Father of all, we give you thanks and praise, that when we were still far off you met us in your Son and brought us home. Dying and living, he declared your love, gave us grace, and opened the gate of glory.

Our Father has met Robert Runcie, and brought him home. In the last sermon in this book, preached in the Chapel Royal, St James's Palace, on New Year's Eve 2000, I set the death of Robert Runcie in the context of Christian hope. That, surely, is where it is right to place it.

I thank my publishers for all the care they have shown, and I thank Jane Spurr for her meticulous care in yet again preparing a manuscript of mine.

Eric James
Easter 2001

Acknowledgements

The author and publishers are grateful to the following for permission to quote from copyright work.

Jonathan Cape for the poem by A. E. Housman, 'Loveliest of trees' in *Collected Poems of A. E. Housman*, 1939.

Faber and Faber for lines from Edwin Muir's poem 'The Transfiguration' in his *Collected Poems 1921–51*, 1952; for lines from T. S. Eliot, *Choruses from 'The Rock'* in his *Collected Poems 1909–62*, 1974; and for three extracts from Dag Hammarskjøld, *Markings*, 1964.

Faber and Faber and the Estate of Siegfried Sassoon for his poem 'They' from *The War Poems*, 1983.

Hodder and Stoughton for verses from Rudyard Kipling's poem 'The Glory of the Garden' in *Rudyard Kipling's Verse*, 1940.

Macmillan and Co. for George William Russell's poem 'Germinal' from his *Collected Poems*, 1917.

PART ONE

Holy Week and Easter 1999

1

Who is This?

Palm Sunday

It is a great privilege for me to share Holy Week with you at St Stephen's, Rochester Row. What I want to say this morning will be more a 'Thought for the Day' than a sermon.

The procession this morning was a very orderly affair. Jesus' entry into Jerusalem, on the first Palm Sunday, was intended to be peaceful. As Mark describes it in his Gospel, Jesus was riding upon an ass, at the beginning of what Christians now call the first Holy Week. But others intended differently, as they often do when there's a procession. The Passover crowds were thronging the streets and, before the week was out, it had all ended in tears and – on Good Friday – violence and bloodshed.

Of course, all that week the political authorities were anxious and, afterwards, there was more than one version of what happened, as there usually is. Some had seen no significance whatever in the palm branches and the ass. Others thought it was a deliberately provocative, anti-authority piece of action. Even today, some biblical scholars think it was calculated to cause the authorities, Jewish and Roman, to view Jesus and his movement as subversive.

Common to all the stories of Jesus' entry into Jerusalem is his going to the Temple, which was like Westminster Abbey is to the Church of England, only more so; but the Temple had its own police force, who would have had their own anxieties. The actions of Jesus' associates, that first Holy Week, make clear that they had *some* idea what they were up to, but never quite understood its full implications. The crowds, we are told, went wild with excitement, and cried, 'Who is this?' Jesus' own disciples were still asking that question. So were the Romans. So were the Jewish hierarchy.

With many other Christians, we shall be asking that question each day this Holy Week: 'Who is this?' – this provocative Jesus we are still thinking about two millennia after he was crucified.

When Robert Runcie was Bishop of St Albans, he asked me, then his Canon Missioner, to stand in for him at a preview of that spectacular film *Jesus of Nazareth*. There was only a handful of us in the private film studio, off Oxford Street. Lord Grade told us that, within six months, 300 million people would have watched that film in the US and Europe. Quite a crowd! A very modern Palm Sunday crowd. That film made you think, 'Who is this?' Certainly it made you think whether the film-makers had got it right; got Jesus right, got 'Who he is' right.

I was with Professor Geoffrey Lampe, a New Testament scholar, in that studio. I remember Lew Grade taking his cigar out of his mouth and putting down his glass of brandy and saying slowly: 'Well, whatever you say, that Jesus is a magnificent man.' Professor Lampe smiled. So did I. We didn't comment, but just let the film go on. I remember thinking at the time that in some of that film, the director, Franco Zeffirelli, seemed to have chosen to copy Rembrandt's idea of Christ and, in other parts, other artists. I found myself thinking that I was only in a position to criticize that film's idea of Christ because I knew in my own mind what my answer was to that question, 'Who is this?' – and why. But my picture of Jesus was, and is, not only made up of what the Bible says about Jesus. It's made up of how I think what the Bible says about Jesus matches and meets my particular needs.

The answer of each one of us to the Palm Sunday question, 'Who is this?' needs to be related to our own needs; and that means that part of our preparation for Holy Week, part of our entry into Holy Week, requires that we spend some time thinking what our needs are, and how they relate to Jesus being crucified.

Crowds of people all over the world will be ignoring Holy Week. But crowds of people will also find themselves suddenly asking afresh this week, 'What has this Jesus and his crucifixion to do with *me*?' And we shall need to have in mind not just our individual needs but the needs of our world, this terrifyingly turbulent world, in which we all feel fairly helpless. And yet the world needs our actions.

I hope you will want to treat that question 'Who is this?' as the question for us all this week. 'Who is this?' for me, at this time; for this church, for our country and for our world today.

Each Holy Week offers each one of us the opportunity to think again: 'Who is this?' – this Jesus. If you can, set aside some time each day to think about that question, wherever you are, at home or at work.

We ask it, not for ourselves alone, but as our intercession for this war-ravaged world.

2

'Who is This?': The Question to his Friends

Monday in Holy Week

Today, let us think about Jesus among his friends, at Bethany, the first day of the first Holy Week. Matthew 26. 1–13 describes one of the most beautiful incidents in our Lord's life, and its beauty and pathos are heightened because we know that tragedy waits in the wings.

Jesus – at Bethany – in the house of 'Simon the leper'. Perhaps the name is witness to some marvel of the healing power of Christ. Perhaps Jesus had helped Simon to live with, come to terms with, his leprosy, with its social stigma. But while Jesus was having a meal with his friends at the house of Simon the leper, a woman came to him with an alabaster jar of the most expensive ointment, and poured it on his head. You can read the story in Mark as well as in Matthew. You can read it in John, but there the woman is named Mary, and her sister Martha is serving; Lazarus is living there, whom Jesus raised from the dead, and Judas is named as the one who objected to what happened.

In St Luke you can read the story in a rather different context. It's a Pharisee's house, and the woman has been living an immoral life. In Luke, it's the feet of Jesus which the woman anoints, not his head. And the host is appalled by the woman touching Jesus. But it's the woman's action which emphasizes the question, 'Who is this?' 'If this man really were a prophet, he would have known who and what sort of woman this is who is touching him.'

In Matthew and Mark, the anointing is to prepare Jesus 'for burial'. It foreshadows and foretells Jesus' death. And Jesus says: 'Wherever in all the world this good news is proclaimed, what she has done will be told also in remembrance of her.'

Well, if all the Gospels had some record of it, with variations, that saying of Jesus is likely to be true. Even today it is one of the most moving stories in all the Gospels; it is a scene that is set before us with the consummate skill of a great artist, a Rembrandt. But the more we look at the scene, the more it comes alive, the more the participants are real, and the more the scene asks questions of us. Do we see the scene as all *men*, apart from this one, rather intrusive, woman? How do we feel about her?

If I give this scene to groups for Bible study, there are usually some who are a bit shocked and embarrassed by this woman. Quite often it is the woman who attracts the question 'Who is this?' to herself. One group said to me, 'It's like a church congregation such as ours being shocked at someone being over-familiar with our vicar!'

'Who is this?' we ask this evening, of Jesus. And the answer from the story must surely be: 'Someone who could evoke this so memorable act of devotion . . . this free act of love.'

As an onlooker of the scene, even with 2000 years between, it's difficult for most of us not to be moved. Here is someone responding to Jesus directly, with a thankful and overflowing heart. The scene is so vividly described that you can almost smell it; but you can see that it stinks in the nostrils of some of the observers. Yet their objection calls forth a soft answer from Jesus. 'Why trouble ye the woman?' It's an extraordinary scene. It takes a Johann Sebastian Bach to cope with it. And those of you who are familiar with the *St Matthew Passion* will know how marvellously Bach has set it to music.

No one would invent this incident. It's a scene of extravagance, of extravagant love. As I read the story, it fills me with admiration and envy, and quite a bit of guilt – that such devotion as I have has a kind of corrupting care about it. I am, frankly, incapable of devotion anything like that to Jesus. There's something in this incident of the flame of God's love, not just a flicker.

But as an onlooker, as I get involved in the scene, I realize that God has, so to speak, put into my hand an alabaster box. Yet where devotion is concerned, I'm a creature of fear, respectability, self-consciousness, self-centredness and, frankly, boredom. A voice within says, 'Prise open the alabaster box,' but it's too much and I'm left moved, but envious of that woman.

'Who is this?' in relation to the alabaster box of devotion which the Lord has put into my hands and yours?

Not so long ago I was asked to preach on 'Why do I pray, and how?' It ought to have been simple, but it was without doubt the most difficult and most searching subject I'd been asked to preach on for several years, or rather, to preach on it honestly.

I had religious parents, and I learned very early on about certain sorts of prayer, and that it was a matter of closing your eyes. It was at least 27 years later that I began to learn very different things about prayer. And now, nearly another 50 years later, grateful as I am for my Methodist upbringing, I would describe my prayer in a very different way from the way prayer was first described to me. I was, in fact, a classic late-developer, and was taken away from school when I was 14, not least because I was such a dunce. I came round to things like Shakespeare at night school, when I was trying to make up for lost time. I remember coming across a phrase in *King Lear* which suddenly seemed to open up new worlds for me, not least new worlds of prayer.

Lear, when he has gone through a lot of suffering, invites his daughter, Cordelia, with him to

> ... take upon's the mystery of things
> As if we were God's spies.

Since, roughly, the time I came across that phrase of Shakespeare, prayer has become to me primarily and overwhelmingly doing just that: taking upon me the mystery of things, as if I were one of God's spies. And I find it important to do that in lots of different ways, at different times and in different places.

Music, for instance, has always meant a lot to me. Listening to it and playing the piano or organ is, for me, often 'taking upon me the mystery of things'. Of course, it means working at getting the notes right. But I don't know what I'd do without music: without music interpreting the 'mystery of things' – not solving it, but plumbing it a bit more, sometimes simply celebrating it. Music has played a large part in my devotional life. My alabaster box is certainly a musical box. You will probably be able to name your own alabaster box.

The work of a priest is very obviously taking upon us the mystery of things – being what St Paul called a 'steward of the mysteries of God'. But I want to suggest that every human being, ordained or lay, is involved in 'taking upon us the mystery of things as if we were God's spies'.

The crescent where I live in South London is backed by ugly high-rise blocks of flats, but at the moment it has a bed of daffodils at its centre and eight trees in bloom. The poet Housman says that 'to look at things in bloom, fifty springs are little room'. From the number of people who take part in our local flower shows I can only believe that many find in the garden and in gardening their alabaster box, and the gateway to the mystery of things.

But this week of all weeks, none of us will need reminding that life isn't all daffodils and almond trees in bloom. The mystery of things includes the mystery of evil as well as of good. And the mystery of evil is quite as profound as the mystery of good.

I was close to Bishop John Robinson, and was privileged to write his biography. I was interested to discover that in only his second sermon, as a deacon, he said that you have to 'discover God in cancer'. Years later, he had to live out those words as he died of cancer.

Mentioning this reminds me how much of my devotional life has related to the mystery of friendship and of human relating. Knowing yourself very close to someone is part of the mystery of things. But sometimes, you're also aware that no matter how close you get, there's a kind of separateness surrounding each one of us. That's also the mystery of things.

Sometimes our sexuality makes us very much like animals, but sometimes we can reverence one another through our sexuality in ways which make us know that sex is one of God's chief ways of enabling us to 'take upon us the mystery of things'. This incident of the woman with the alabaster box ought to say something to us of a devotion and worship which includes and takes up our sexuality. Our sexuality is part of our alabaster box.

My day-to-day job for several years was to run a charity called Christian Action. People often asked me what it did, and I would say that it was to do with justice and peace. And I'd often add that Archbishop William Temple used to say that 'justice is the first requirement of love'. I wanted people to see that when you deal with love and justice, you take upon yourself the mystery of things, but you have to do it in very down-to-earth ways, such as in bringing up a family and housing them. Devotion to justice and peace is all in the alabaster box.

The heart of the mystery for Christians is, of course, the eventually triumphant suffering of Jesus. It's the best spy-hole on the mystery. As we think upon the pain of Christ, we get close to the pain of the world, and wherever we encounter that, we find that the pain of Christ interprets it and profoundly comments upon this mystery of things. And every time we come to the eucharist, that mystery is set before us.

I want to read you a passage from Professor John Macquarrie on 'Mystery and Truth'. He says:

> There is today a revival of interest in mystery and the sense of wonder in our secular society, especially among young people. This may mark the beginning of a revulsion against the long established hostility to mystery in Western philosophy. Now if it is true that the most natural (though not the only) way into mystery is through the exploration of man himself, then the Christian faith is singularly well-situated to give a lead in the quest for mystery. By its doctrine of the incarnation, Christianity holds that it is precisely in a human person, Jesus Christ, that the final mystery of being has been opened up. According to Paul, Christ is 'the revelation of the mystery which was kept secret for long ages' (Rom. 16.25–6). This is commonly taken to mean that Christ has revealed or has opened up the mystery of God. But would it not be correct to say that he has done this by opening up the mystery of man? Is there not a deep affinity between the mystery of God and the mystery of humanity? By becoming man in the fullest sense, that is to say, in a measure of fullness that transcends all our ordinary levels of manhood, Christ manifests God in the flesh. He pushes back the horizons of the human mystery so that they open on to the divine mystery, but he does this without ceasing to be man.

It's in response to the divine mystery in our humanity that we are invited to prize open the alabaster box of our hearts, our feelings, all that we are, body, mind and soul.

Let me remind you where we began this evening. I asked, 'Who is this?', and I said that on this first day of Holy Week we find Jesus among his friends, at Bethany. So that when we ask the question 'Who is this?', we find that he is a man who needs friends, values friendship. I learned quite a lot about friendship when I was here as a curate in the 1950s, and I think that friendship is the most important thing in life for me. I love the saying of Aelred of Rievaulx: 'God is friendship.'

'Who is this?' He is the revelation of God as friendship, of God in friendship.

'Who is this?' This Monday in Holy Week I want to answer: He is the one who enables us who are human to prize open the mysterious alabaster box that is uniquely ours. But I want you to be able to make your own answer to that question, your own response – with the mysterious alabaster box which is uniquely yours.

He who has opened up our human relationship is the one who has opened up our relationship with him. Each of us, as part of our very creation and our own relationships, has this unique alabaster box put into our hands, and it's for us to use, not least this very week.

3

'Who is This?': The Question for Those who Betray him

Tuesday in Holy Week

Today's Gospel reading (Matt. 26.14–75) began with Peter's assertion that he would never lose faith in Jesus, in who he is, followed by Jesus' prophecy that Peter will disown him. Then followed Gethsemane, when the disciples slept. And then came Judas, with his band of men and the chief priests and elders. Judas betrayed Jesus with a kiss. Shortly after, Peter denied Jesus – three times. It's a tragic tale.

The crucifixion, and all that led up to it is, you might say, a study in betrayal. And the full truth of that we shall hear in the Gospel reading tomorrow, when St Matthew records the question our Lord does not simply *ask* from the cross, but *cries out* with every fibre of his being: 'My God, my God, why hast *thou* forsaken me?'

The human betrayals are but the circumference of the Passion. The heart and centre of it is the seeming betrayal by God himself. The body of the betrayal is the disciples' betrayal. The soul of the betrayal is the sense of betrayal by God. Jesus is the very personification of the seemingly God-forsaken. It is important in Holy Week to penetrate, as far as we can, Christ's experience of betrayal, human and divine, if we are to penetrate to the depths of who he is.

There is a Jewish story which tells of a father and his son on the boy's seventh birthday. 'My son,' says the father, 'your seventh birthday is a very important day in the life of a Jewish boy. You're really grown up now. And there's a very special game for a father and son to play together this particular day. Come here,' the father says, 'I want you to jump from the bottom stair and I'll catch you.' The boy jumps, and the father catches him. Then he places him on the second stair, and says, 'Jump, and I'll catch you.' And so on with the third, fourth, fifth and sixth stair. Each time, the boy jumps, and the father catches him. When he comes to the seventh stair, the father says: 'The *seventh* stair, on your *seventh* birthday, is very special. It's the very sign that you're grown up, my son. Jump, and I'll catch you.' The boy jumps because he trusts his father. But this time the father steps aside, and the boy falls flat on his face. As he picks himself up, bleeding and crying, he screams to his father: 'Daddy, why did you move away?' And the father says to him: 'Son, the most loving thing I can do for you on your seventh birthday, now you're grown up, is to teach you never to trust anyone, not even your own father.'

It's a terrible, terrible story, which I can hardly bear to tell. But, of course, it contains a terrible truth. The Passion of our Lord is about betrayal. Is the heart of it the Father's betrayal of the Son? Did the Father step aside, as the sign of the Son's full humanity?

From Christ's question 'My God, my God, why hast thou forsaken me?' you might at first think so, and not only at first. Those words are the first words of Psalm 22. The story I've told you is a comment on those words from the psalm. There are many human cries of agony, down the ages and across the world, many cries of 'My God, my God, why hast thou forsaken me?' – maybe in Kosovo today - cries from the utter loneliness of betrayal.

Some of you will have read the short book called *Night*, an autobiographical fragment by the Hungarian Jew, Elie Wiesel, who was deported with his family from Auschwitz when he was still a boy, to Buchenwald. A rabbi who teaches Elie to pray, as a youth in the concentration camp, explains to him that every question possesses a power that does not lie simply in what seems the obvious and immediate answer. 'Man raises himself toward God,' he says, 'by the questions he asks him. Man questions and God answers. But we don't understand his answers. I pray to God within me,' says the rabbi, 'that he will give me the strength to ask him the right questions.'

On the cross, Christ has the strength to ask the right question. Asking God the right questions is a very good definition not only of prayer, but of our whole relationship to God, the God who is within, above and utterly beyond us. And Jesus' question is the very pattern of that prayer and that relationship. St Thomas Aquinas, commenting on our Lord's cry to his Father, says: 'God withdrew his protection but did not break the union.' There will be times in this life for almost all of us when it *seems* that God has withdrawn his protection. It is then we most need to trust, to have faith that he has not broken the union between ourselves and the Father. And we need to go on in that faith, in that trust, in that understanding. That is what Jesus did.

It's possible to think of many people today who through one circumstance and another will *feel* God has withdrawn his protection. I mention again the refugees fleeing from Kosovo, fatherless and homeless. Or it may be some experience of betrayal in some personal relationship. It may be *seeming* betrayal through some physical suffering, disability, or some circumstance like the loss of a job, or the loss of a baby, a husband, a wife, a mother, or a father. Bereave-ment is often first experienced as betrayal. Almost every broken marriage or partnership has *some* sense of betrayal at the heart of it. And there are some people who grieve for what they have never and can never have, for instance, a baby. Homelessness may be experienced as betrayal. Racial prejudice may be experienced as betrayal; the mental illness of one's children or dependants; AIDS. Even retirement can feel like betrayal; you're bereaved of the status, the identity, you once possessed.

In Morris West's novel, *The Clowns of God*, the Professor's young son says to him: 'We were angry with you and your generation because you had a past to look back on, while we had only a question mark to look forward to.' Bereaved of the future, betrayed by the shape of existence itself.

When I was a curate here, I used to run a lunch-time discussion group in what was then the Colonial Office, on Millbank. I read a lecture called 'Creative Suffering' given at Lincoln Theological College, by someone called Julia de Beausobre. I then read her autobiography, with the title *The Woman Who Could Not Die* – her reminiscences of life in a Russian concentration camp, of which that lecture was the fruit. I thought I would ask her to come and talk to my discussion group. I found her phone number and dialled it, and was surprised to hear the woman at the other end say, 'Lady Namier speaking.' Thinking I'd got a wrong number, I said: 'I'm sorry, I wanted someone with the ridiculous name of Julia de Beausobre.' 'I am she,' she replied, with the perfect English of a foreigner. When I'd recovered, I explained what I wanted of her. She said she would not give a talk, but if I would like to interview her she would be happy to answer my questions. She said she would arrive by taxi at the junction of Great Peter Street and Millbank. When she alighted from the taxi, I was astonished by her radiance – knocked back by it.

Her first husband had been killed in the concentration camp. She herself had been appallingly tortured. So I had expected to meet someone emaciated and crushed. But she had a remarkable radiance, dignity and stillness. It was the simplicity of what she had to say that astonished me. It was as though she had pared everything down to its essentials. When I asked her how she survived in the camp, she replied: 'It was simple, really. I tried to love my torturers, because if I loved them I would not be adding to the evil in the world, and they would not have succeeded in adding to the evil in the world by making me hate them. But if I loved, it just could be that it might have some effect on them, and even reduce the amount of evil in the world. So,' she said, 'at the simplest level of prudence, Christ's way of love and trust and forgiveness seemed to be the only way – Christ's way of love, in oneness with the Father.' Of course, Julia de Beausobre did not always *feel* the Father's protection. She acted in *faith* in the unbroken union.

Holy Week teaches us much about betrayal; about man's inhumanity to man, about corruption among disciples in church and state, about corruption within ourselves, about the betrayal within ourselves which gets coagulated with the betrayal of others into the betrayal of the church. But we call it *Holy* Week and *Good* Friday because Jesus revealed the creative possibilities *within* our capacities for betrayal and our acts of betrayal. Those creative possibilities, revealed supremely in the cross and resurrection, revealed in the church and the world, we call Redemption. The Creator-Redeemer God can renew in us again and again the faith that can transform individuals, not least ourselves; can transform families, the church, the world. That's who our Creator-Redeemer God is, and whom his Son revealed the first Holy Week. That's 'Who he is.'

When I was a student, I spent one Holy Week at Mirfield, with the Community of the Resurrection. The Superior then, Father Talbot, gave an address on the words: 'The same night that he was betrayed, Jesus took bread.' He asked us, 'Have you yet had any experience of betrayal?' He looked around him. We were all young students. He went on, 'Maybe you haven't yet, but I expect you will have. Remember then, that on the same night he was betrayed, he took bread. At the worst time, he did the best deed. He used his betrayal as the means of redemption. If Jesus did that, so can you – in his power. Do not be embittered by betrayal. Use it as the means of redemption.' Then he quoted that wonderful inscription over the porch of the church at Staunton Harold, in Leicestershire, which was built at the time of the Commonwealth in 1653. It simply says:

> When throughout the nation all things sacred were either demolished or profaned, this church was founded by Sir Robert Shirley, Baronet, whose singular praise it is to have done the best things in the worst time and hoped them in the most calamitous.

Who is this? A man betrayed. *The* Man betrayed. But a man of unconquerable faith and hope. He said: 'My God, my God, Why?' But it is still, '*My* God'. In the darkness, he still said, '*My* God'. I repeat the question Father Talbot asked me: 'Have you had any experience of betrayal yet?'

Not long before I was ordained, my Dean at King's College, Eric Abbott, said to me: 'Boy, you're a romantic, and you won't survive unless you have a very high doctrine of corruption, in church as well as state.' For many years, I simply didn't know what he meant. And then, all of a sudden, I did, at the beginning of the 1970s. The details don't matter; but I experienced from good men in the church, from people in very high positions of responsibility, black evil. I learned in those months more about betrayal than I'd ever known or am ever likely to know and, as I say, in the church. The romantic in me simply did not know what had hit me. But, in a curious way, I look back on those events now, a good many years after, as the best thing that ever happened to me. When I was in the midst of it all, I went abroad for some months and I asked the bishop there if I could see his wisest priest. He sent me to quite a young priest, who said to me: 'You must not expect to see any resolution of this situation on this side of the grave. You must simply commit it to God, and treat any resolution in this life as a bonus.' Well, there have been a lot of bonuses. Coming here this week, and feeling I'm among friends, and being invited to preach about 'Who is he?', he who used his betrayal as a means of redemption: that's all bonus.

Of course, the basic saving element in such circumstances is the sense: 'If I go down into Hell thou are there also,' and 'You've been there, Jesus, before me and deeper, far deeper; and you've been raised from the depths and can raise me.'

Poetry has helped me a lot over the years. The Irish poet George William Russell, who used the pseudonym AE, wrote a poem called 'Germinal', which ends with these six lines:

> In ancient shadows and twilights
> Where childhood had strayed,
> The world's great sorrows were born
> And its heroes were made.
> In the lost childhood of Judas
> Christ was betrayed.

There's something of a lost childhood, and something of a Judas, in us all. But it is never too late for love's redeeming work to be done with the Judas in us. It's been done *for* us. Now it needs to be done *in* us.

A poem by the Scottish poet, Edwin Muir, called 'The Transfiguration' has within it these marvellous ten lines:

> Then he will come, Christ the uncrucified,
> Christ the discrucified, his death undone,
> His agony unmade, his cross dismantled –
> Glad to be so – and the tormented wood
> Will cure its hurt and grow into a tree
> In a green springing corner of young Eden,
> And Judas damned take his long journey backward
> From darkness into light and be a child
> Beside his mother's knee, and the betrayal
> Be quite undone and never more be done.

'Who is this?' A man who experienced betrayal to the full but did all that could be done, all that needed to be done, with its raw material.

But I have been constantly learning that this theme of betrayal also has a great deal of danger in it. If the church encourages people to sing hymns that say:

> Who was the guilty? Who brought this upon thee?
> Alas, my treason, Jesu, hath undone thee.
> 'Twas I, Lord Jesu. I it was denied thee.
> I crucified thee.

there is considerable danger. There's of course much truth there, but it must be carefully handled. And what must be said with great clarity and power – what must be the overwhelming message – is not of 'my betrayal' but of God's love.

Dr Jack Dominian, the Roman Catholic psychiatrist and writer, has this passage in his recent book, a psychological interpretation of Jesus which he called *One Like Us*:

Both Peter and Judas had betrayed Jesus. Why did one reconcile himself to the fact, weep and be ready to pick up the relationship of love again, while the other hanged himself? This is a psychological question. Peter had within himself the remnants of genuine love, not exhausted by his betrayal. His emotional attachment to Jesus stood fast, and so there was a lifeline between them which was not erased by the betrayal. The personality is made up of several layers, and deep inside him, Peter had an honest love for Jesus which, although it was temporarily subdued by fear, was not extinguished. The attachment of affection remained.

Judas also felt remorse – but the next layer of his being revealed the enmity, the emptiness, the antipathy, that he felt towards Jesus. It was this antipathy that motivated his betrayal – unlike Peter's betrayal, which was based on fear. Judas could not tolerate Jesus' invocation of love. It was foreign to him. When he recognized his betrayal he had, unlike Peter, nothing to fall back on. The next layer of his being was emptiness. He had nothing to cherish and so his life had no meaning . . .

Judas and Peter are important prototypes for all of us. Both betrayed Jesus after extended intimacy with him. We too betray Jesus in a variety of ways. Judas felt that there was no way back. For him, the only possible outcome was despair. For Peter, there was a retracing of his steps, remorse and personal reconciliation. That is the way that we have to follow. No matter how often we betray Jesus by not loving, there is always a chance to return to loving him.

'Who is this?' One like us.

4

'Who is This?': Jesus on Trial

Wednesday in Holy Week

Matthew 27.1–56 describes how, when morning came, all the chief priests and elders of the people met in council to bring about the death of Jesus. They had him bound, and led him away, to hand him over to Pilate, the Governor. The Gospel goes on to describe how Jesus conducted himself before Pilate. He is more silent, according to Matthew, than he was before the chief priests and the Sanhedrin, but not so in John's account. Our Lord's example is sometimes quoted as a back-up for a kind of Christian-pacifism-in-all-circumstances. I Peter 2.23 says that he did not answer back with insult; when he suffered, he did not threaten.

Last evening, I spoke of the example of Julia de Beausobre, and of how greatly I admire her example of submission, in the power of Christ; a submission to her torturers in the concentration camp that was positive, indeed loving. I believe there's a major subject here which every Christian has to confront, and that is: what validity, and what value, has the marvellous phrase of Thomas à Kempis, 'The Imitation of Christ'? In what areas is it appropriate and in what inappropriate? In what areas is it possible and in what impossible?

We can't tackle that in any detail now, but it is crucial. I shall take it for granted that the example of Christ before his accusers is highly relevant to what I will call our 'confrontational situations' in our personal life and in the national and international situations where we have to work at peace and justice in our world today. We cannot just sit here, having pious thoughts, while our politicians and others confront the real world on our behalf in, say, Northern Ireland and Kosovo. But, for the moment, I simply underline that the question 'Is

Jesus someone we can and should *imitate*?' is very relevant to our question, 'Who is this?' And I think it's very important in Holy Week for our picture of Christ not to be selective.

There are some words of our Lord which I have myself only preached on once in my 48 years of ordained ministry, and which I've never heard anyone else preach on and which are certainly not pacific words. I mean the words of our Lord in relation to Herod: 'Go tell that fox ...'

'Who is this?' The man who stood up to and confronted Herod. The man who, in his innocence and utter integrity and guiltlessness, stood up to Herod – as he would to Pilate and the chief priests, in different ways. And let us not forget those other words from the Palm Sunday Gospel:

> Jesus went into the Temple and drove out all who were buying and selling in the Temple precincts; he upset the tables of the money changers and the seats of the dealers in pigeons and told them that they were making the Temple a robber's cave (Matt. 21.12–13).

I said on Sunday that, to the Jews, the Temple was something like a combination of Westminster Abbey and Scotland Yard. It was certainly a seat of authority, of politics as well as religion.

'Who is this?' It's the man of peace who disturbed the peace of Jerusalem, the City of Peace, on the first day of the first Holy Week; that is to say, at its most vulnerable time, when everyone was up for the Passover, when the Gospel recorded 'There must be no disturbance among the people during the festivities', and when the place was at its most crowded. (And even John puts the cleansing of the Temple at Passover time.) It's no surprise that people like Martin Luther King and Mahatma Gandhi have found in Jesus the inspiration and example of their political actions. Jesus before Pilate and Caiaphas is an example – I would say, an icon – of confrontation. But we may not be romantic in our imitation of Christ.

To Milton and Shakespeare, to protest meant to proclaim, to affirm, to vow, to witness. 'Seeing we are compassed about with so great a cloud of witnesses' (Heb. 12.1): the Greek word there for witness is *marturos*. Martyrs, witnesses, proclaimers, protesters all have, or should have, much in common. As I see it, in the very midst of the cloud of witnesses, for the Christian, stands:

Jesus Christ, the martyr for peace, justice and reconciliation;
Jesus Christ, the witness to peace, justice and reconciliation;
Jesus Christ: the proclaimer of peace, justice and reconciliation;
Jesus Christ: the protester for peace, justice and reconciliation;
Jesus Christ; the one who confronts the politicians Herod, Annas,
Caiaphas, Pilate and others more anonymous.

And seeing Christ there, and in that way, we may see that protest for
the Christian, not least political protest, must be fundamentally
positive, not negative; fundamentally affirmative, at cost, at risk,
grounded in the great and central truths of the Christian faith – the
truths of our creation in love, all of us; the truths of our nature and
destiny; the truths of that love which is the origin, sustenance,
redemption, completion and goal of us all, grounded in the creative
and redeeming love Jesus in his whole ministry reveals his Father to
be. The motive of protest for the Christian must always be anchored
in him whose nature and whose name is love.

But what about the means and method of protest? Does the
example of Christ at Passiontide have anything to say to us here? Does
it invite imitation?

In the fourteenth-century mystical writings called the *Theologia
Germanica* there is this passage:

> He said to Judas when he had betrayed him: 'Friend, wherefore art
> thou come?' Just as if he had said: 'Thou hatest me, and art mine
> enemy, yet I love thee and am thy friend.' As though God in human
> nature were saying: 'I am pure, simple Goodness, and therefore I
> cannot will or desire or rejoice in or do or give anything but goodness.
> If I am to reward thee for thy evil and wickedness, I must do it with
> goodness, for I am and have nothing else.'

Yes: but the precise means and method? What about that?

In his *Life of Christ* the French novelist François Mauriac has a
marvellous description of Christ cleansing the Temple. He describes
him with a whip of small cords in his hands, the sweat pouring off his
face. And then he adds this powerful sentence: 'Nobody that day
could tell he was love.' But his point is that he *was* love – love with a
whip of small cords in his hands. Mauriac's whole point is that he was
– is – love, in spite of appearances. The means and the method of
Christian protest will always be the means and method of love, in
spite of appearances.

In the Second World War, when I was 'out of work', as they say, before ordination, I heard William Temple, then Archbishop of Canterbury, preach a lunch-time sermon in St Mary Woolnoth in the City of London. He had been asked to preach on 'How can a Christian take part in war?' Temple had probably been a pacifist for much of his life and had only edged his way into a more militarist position, painfully and reluctantly, but in that sermon on political responsibility at that time, I remember a vivid sentence: 'Which is more loving,' Temple asked, 'to kill two million Germans to save ten million Jews or to keep your powder dry?' At that time the nature of the Holocaust was only just becoming clear – that the Germans were bent on virtual genocide where the Jews were concerned. But it was interesting that Temple used, that day, the almost antique phrase, 'keep your powder dry'. It was as if he could not quite bring himself to face what weapons modern war was actually requiring if we were to win the war and stop the slaughter of Jews: he could not bring himself to describe the realities of, for instance, obliteration bombing. (The nuclear bomb was then still in the future.)

In his own way, Temple was pointing out that, in this world, human choices – not least political choices – are often a choice of the lesser of two evils. The person who thinks he has clean hands and a pure heart because he has not taken up arms may be a self-deceiving idealist who has not taken seriously enough the permanent and inescapable relation between love and power, and the compromise and compromising decisions that inevitably involves.

Christians have, at every stage, in every situation, to weigh their actions in, so to speak, the balance of love. What is the most loving thing to be done at this moment? And there is no easy method of computation which will guarantee that we have the right answer. At this moment it may be wrong to take this action or that. Now there is still time for negotiation, for some creative act of reconciliation. But how can you be sure that the creative act of trust will not be taken as – and in fact will not be – the fatal act of weakness? You cannot be certain. There is never an act of faith without risk. Yes, but too much risk, if you're risking someone else's survival, can be as unloving as too little. And too little may be as unloving as too much. Nelson Mandela went through agonies before he reluctantly decided the ANC must use some violence. So Christ's 'confrontations' have something to say to us on the motive of protest and, I think, on the means and method of protest. But I think it is clear that they also say something about the moment of protest.

Jesus often talked about his 'hour', and particularly as his cross and Passion drew near. 'Mine hour is not yet come.' There was a time as well as a place for the cleansing of the Temple and Jesus deliberately chose it. He went up to Jerusalem. The geographical choice, the choice of place, was made with deliberation, but at a particular time: the Passover. He had a responsible strategy of human choice, of human decision. The right moment for political protest is always very important indeed.

At the height of Nazi power, Dietrich Bonhoeffer and his friend Eberhard Bethge were in a café when the news of the Fall of France came over the loudspeaker, and there were many Nazi salutes. Bethge was horrified and distressed to see Bonhoeffer giving the salute with apparent vigour. Bonhoeffer laughed and said, 'Put up your arm! This thing – a mere salute – isn't worth dying for!' But a few years later Bonhoeffer's 'hour' had come, the moment for action that almost inescapably led to martyrdom. Paul Schneider, the first martyr of the Confessing Church in Germany, instinctively resisted, and died in a way that reads like the Acts of the Apostles. Such men were and are needed in the church and in the world. There's a different way of the cross for different Christians. Bonhoeffer had another task which, while it risked martyrdom, did not require it immediately. His hour had not yet come.

You will have observed that as a mnemonic, for purposes of memory, I have spoken of motive, method, means and moment. I'm going to cheat a little at this point and add another 'm': 'minute particulars'! You may know the poet William Blake's phrase: 'He who would do good to another must do it in minute particulars' – in down-to-earth details. He goes on to say that the 'general good is the plea of the scoundrel, hypocrite and flatterer'. Well, the way people sometimes talk of Jesus, you'd think he was simply a 'general good' merchant. And the way people often interpret following the example of Jesus, you'd think it is simply to be concerned with the general good.

It is important to say that protest is often a luxury unless you have thought out your objectives in minute particulars and are willing to take on the detailed work involved in gaining those objectives and holding on to them. Power, in subordination to love, requires just as much attention to minute particulars as power that is not in subordination to love.

I want to add just one more 'm' to the list. You may think it is a somewhat strange bedfellow: 'm' for modesty. As you look at Christ before his accusers, you look at innocence and even infallibility. But not a kind of ready-made, reach-me-down, infallibility, off the peg. Infallibility is really an eschatological virtue. It belongs to the next world, not this, nor to the church in this world – only to Christ and to the kingdom of Christ.

Go through the dialogues of the Passion this week. Christ before Pilate says: 'For this cause came I into the world, that I should bear witness unto the truth. Everyone that is of the truth heareth my voice.' Pilate says to him: 'What is truth?' And then he goes out to the crowd and says, 'I find no fault in him.'

Christ was utterly confident of the truth. 'Who is this?' One who had confidence in the truth. But for us there are very few situations in which genuine modesty is not appropriate and does not strengthen our case – our case, not least, for peace and justice.

For, as St Paul said, 'now we know in part'. That doesn't mean a kind of lily-livered liberal 'there's truth in every position' which never allows us to take decisive action, but a consciousness that we, none of us, ever have a monopoly of truth. I do not think that in the years that lie ahead Christians will be less in situations of confrontation than hitherto. So I commend to you for further consideration, meditation and confrontation – after the example and in the power of our Lord Jesus Christ – motive, means, method, moment, minute particulars and modesty.

At the beginning of our thinking together, we used words that might sound a little forbidding to some: martyr; witness; protest; confrontation – all in relation to Jesus confronting Herod, Annas, Caiaphas and Pilate. Such words sound forbidding because we don't see ourselves doing that sort of thing.

May I remind you that, in the ordinary life of the church, we are never very far from these words. Every time I baptize a baby, I use a phrase of the Victorian theologian F. D. Maurice, who said: 'Baptism is the proclamation by God that this child is a child of mine.' You can't proclaim that, you can't witness to that fact, and leave that child homeless or the victim of racial prejudice. You can't be casual about the kind of hospital care it will have. This very night, we can't proclaim Kosovans children of God and abandon them. Nor indeed can we bomb the Serbs regardless – regardless of the fact that we proclaim them to be children of God.

Jesus on trial confronts us all.

5

'Who is This?': The Question at the Last Supper

Maundy Thursday

I wonder: have you ever set your heart on having a party with friends, and made all sorts of preparations, gone to endless trouble, and then, when the evening has come, it has all gone hopelessly wrong and ended in tears? I think the first Maundy Thursday must have been something like that, not least, of course, for Jesus.

What's certain is that he'd given a lot of thought to the meal he was going to have with his disciples who, significantly, he simply called his 'friends'. Whether it was the Passover meal itself – as the first three Gospels say it was – or whether it was one of the preparatory meals that often preceded a Jewish festival and every sabbath, Jesus had taken a great deal of care over it. It was very much his party. He'd made very careful arrangements with a friend, and the disciples had gone into Jerusalem to complete the preparations. Eventually, Jesus had joined them, and at first, everything had gone as he'd planned.

And then, at that moment of all moments, at that meal of all meals, a row had broken out among the disciples as to which of them was 'top dog'. It was heart-breaking for Jesus. But he didn't tear them off a strip. Actions speak louder than words, so he simply took a towel and a basin of water, and began to wash their feet, saying, 'Look! I've done this as something for you to follow. If you do what I've done, if you wash one another's feet, there can't possibly be any of this "top dog" nonsense.'

But that row wasn't the only thing that went wrong that evening. It was at that meal that it finally became clear – to Jesus at least – that Judas was going to betray him. In fact, it was clear to Jesus that the end could not now be far off. The disciples' row; Judas' betrayal; the end at hand. What an evening!

The disciples were startled beyond words when Jesus began to wash their feet. But there was something even more startling to come. The kind of meal they were accustomed to having together was something which as Jews they were very used to. It had its regular pattern and ritual. But what Jesus suddenly said, in the middle of the meal, was unbelievable.

They all knew that the meal they were having celebrated the time when, centuries before, God had delivered their nation from slavery. But, suddenly, Jesus said words that implied, unmistakably, that God had established a new relationship between himself and humanity: a new Covenant, through him, through Jesus himself; through his blood; his life; his suffering; and his death, still ahead. It was as he gave thanks and took bread – there was no surprise about that – that he suddenly said the revolutionary words, 'This is my Body, which is for you. Do this in remembrance of me.' And when he took the cup, he said, 'This is the New Covenant, sealed by my own Blood. Do this, as often as you drink it, in remembrance of me.' They all knew about the Old Covenant between God and Israel. But their 'Master' was saying, 'This is the New Covenant in and through my Blood.' It was either the most incredible arrogance, or nonsense, or madness, or blasphemy – or the truth.

But they knew very well that the man who had just washed their feet wasn't arrogant – far from it, and he wasn't mad, or blasphemous. They knew he was a man of profound prayer, and goodness. Hadn't they watched him at prayer, often enough, early in the morning? It was the terrible and glorious events of the next few days which filled out for them what Jesus had meant by his words and actions at the table that evening. But it was with heavy hearts that they sang a hymn together, some no doubt near to tears, and went out with Jesus to the Garden of Gethsemane.

Several years later, St Paul was writing to the church at Corinth. Believe it or not, among other things the Corinthians had been up to, they had been getting drunk at holy communion. St Paul decided to write them a letter in which he described what he had been told had happened that very first Maundy Thursday. And here we are now, nearly two millennia later, keeping Maundy Thursday evening; having a part of St Paul's letter read again, and the description in St John's Gospel of that first Last Supper.

In our churches today we tend to separate off our meetings from our services, and no longer does our communion service look all that much like a meal together. I think we lose quite a bit through that, but at least no one dreams of having a row, as the disciples did, at holy communion.

But in these days, when the McDonald's sign is becoming better known than the cross, and when people no longer sit down together at the meal table, the church must surely set the world an example afresh – Catholic and Protestant, Serbian Orthodox and Kosovan – anticipating the kingdom come. But if it is to be an example to the world, it has to be again essentially a group of disciples, of friends, who gather round a table, knowing that it is the Lord himself who has prepared the meal, that it is the Lord who himself passes to each one of us the bread and cup to share with one another, and says to each one of us, 'This is my Body. This is my Blood.' A shared loaf and a shared cup is the very essence of holy communion; literally, the heart of the matter.

Not long ago, I came across a poem which I think may have something special to say to us on Maundy Thursday evening. It's by Chuck Lathrop, a Canadian, and it's called 'In Search of a Roundtable'.

> Concerning the why and how and what and who
> of ministry,
> one image keeps surfacing:
> A table that is round.
>
> It will take some sawing
> to be roundtabled,
> some redefining
> and redesigning,
> some redoing and rebirthing
> of narrowlong Churching
> can painful be
> for people and tables.
> It would mean no daising
> and throning,
> for but one king is there,
> and he was a footwasher,
> at table no less.
>
> And what of narrowlong ministers
> when they confront
> a roundtable people,

after years of workng up the table
to finally sit at its head,
only to discover
that the table has been turned round?

They must be loved into roundness,
for God has called a People,
not 'them and us'.
'Them and us'
are unable
to gather round;
for at a roundtable,
there are no sides
and ALL are invited
to wholeness and to food.

At one time
our narrowing Churches
were built to resemble the cross
but it does no good
for buildings to do so,
if lives do not.

Roundtabling means
no preferred seating,
no first and last,
no better, and no corners
for the 'least of these'.
Roundtabling means
being with,
a part of,
together, and one.
It means room for the Spirit
and gifts
and disturbing profound peace for all.

We can no longer prepare for the past.
We will and must and are called
to be Church,
and if He calls for other than roundtable
we are bound to follow.

Leaving the sawdust
and chips, designs and redesigns
behind,

in search of and in the presence of
the Kingdom
that is His and not ours.
Amen.

'Who is this?' He who from the first Last Supper until now has been in search of and gathering his roundtable church.

6

Good Friday 1: Thinking about the Cross

I think it's always right on Good Friday to address ourselves first to a very simple question: 'Why am I here today?' Why are we, and so many of our fellow Christians, spending this time 'thinking about the cross?' We don't spend much time thinking about the death of, say, Francis of Assisi. In the end, I think, there's only one answer: that we believe St Paul spoke truly when he wrote 'God was in Christ . . .' We believe St John spoke truly when he wrote that 'God so loved the world that he gave his only begotten Son . . .'

But I don't think even those statements are enough in themselves. It's not enough to say that 'God was in Christ . . .' if all that remains is a far-off thing of long ago, a 2000-year-old event. Most of us, I imagine, only want to be here today if we can be taken further into the mystery of existence *today*: the mystery of our own existence, and the mystery of the world's existence.

'Thinking about the cross' is very different from simply thinking about another event in history. The cross *was* that, but, as T. S. Eliot wrote:

> Then came, at a predetermined moment, a moment in time and of time,
> A moment not out of time, but in time, in what we call history: transecting, bisecting the world of time, a moment in time but not like a moment of time,
> A moment in time but time was made through that moment: for without the meaning there is no time, and that moment of time gave the meaning.

Because that moment 'gave the meaning', thinking about the cross means most of all discovering the cross at the heart of our own everyday experience, our own selves; discovering the cross-like self-giving of God at the very heart of our own existence and experience. It greatly helps me to begin to think of the cross with my own experience.

It is a common human experience to want to share the things we have, the best things we know in life. 'You must read the book I've just read,' we say. Or, 'You must see the film I've just seen.' The desire to share is, I think, at the heart of being human. I cannot myself believe that this heart of humanity is a meaningless part of our existence. I believe it witnesses to something, to a recognizably personal source of our life. And this personal origin of life is confirmed, focused, made blazingly clear, in Jesus. In his life and, supremely, in his cross, in his triumphant suffering, he witnesses to and mirrors this personal meaning and origin of things, and to its nature.

This is what St Paul means when he says that 'God was in Christ,' and when St John says 'God so loved that he gave . . .' This loving, this giving, this sharing has been true of God right from eternity, not just for 2000 years. God is love. And because God is love, love like the cross, he creates. He shares. He shares himself. He shares the good that he is; all the good that he knows, he shares. For him not to have shared would have been to stop being who he is.

So, at the very heart of our common human experience, there is this profound indication, this pointer, this deep experience of what life is about. We understand, deep down, from our own experience, our own roots, our own depths, that it is of the very nature of love to share and create. And at the very heart of our experience, not only of how the world is made but that it is made at all, we understand what, in Christ, God has said so explicitly: that he is love, love like the cross. And out of his love, and for his love, and to share his love, he has made us, each one of us, and all the world.

As Bishop Walsham How's hymn 'It is a thing most wonderful' says, very simply:

> But even could I see him die,
> I could but see a little part
> Of that great love, which, like a fire,
> Is always burning in his heart.

Out of that fire of his love, God made man: God sustains man, and all the world. And we, in our human experiences, have deep intimations of that central truth.

But think what that means. It means that we cannot 'think about the cross' as simply a day, an event, in the past, fairly remote from our twentieth century and all its ways, customs and habits. It means that we are to see all the powers of creation, around us and within us, as in some way streaming from the cross itself, from the cross in the very heart of God.

But, if that be the truth, we shall begin to see the ordinary as extraordinary, and as a cause for wonder. We shall be struck by the ordinary; by the fact that I am, that I am who I am, that a tree is itself, that there is anything at all. We shall, with awe and wonder, revalue creation, revalue life, revalue ourselves, revalue all our relationships, revalue all God's people. We shall revalue all God's world as God's shared gift, as God sharing himself.

In the beginning, God was the God who was in Christ, like Christ, forever sharing who he ever was, and is, and shall be. Therefore, the hot dense furnace which became our universe millions of years ago, came to be. And thousands of millions of years later, this earth came to be. Then, within this earth, life came to be. Millions of years later, vertebrates came to be, then reptiles, then mammals, then anthropoids; and in as it were the very last second of the very last hour of the one day that forms the whole lifespan of this universe – man came to be, through God, who is like Christ, sharing who he ever was and is.

Through this cross-like love-in-creation, man has been continually emerging from the little dark creature with the pebble, the flint and the knife and the spear in his hand, to become the artist, the mathematician, the scientist, the city builder, the space-traveller, the politician, the musician, the friend, the homemaker, the priest, the cook, the discoverer of who-he-is and who God is.

And, 2000 years ago, men of Palestine beheld 'the Man', Jesus Christ, our Lord. In the last half-hour of the one day that is the whole lifespan of man on the earth, Jesus came to be, into the midst of this so tiny fragment of the history of creation, through him who was, and is, and ever shall be, the God of the cross. So when today we 'think about the cross', we have to see ourselves, our own creation, as God sharing himself. All we are comes from the pure stream of God's creative love flowing from the cross in the heart of God himself.

All the energies of sex, parenthood, our power to create, our power to have children and bring them up, our power to have friends and love them, our power to look after people, to look after those who have no friends; our gifts of language, of asking questions about ourselves, of penetrating the deepest levels of reality, of creation, of knowing good and evil; all music, art, poetry, television, technology – there is something in all these which is from the cross in the heart of God.

And if all these things are from the cross in the heart of God, it's not strange that they should mean so much to us. It's not strange that those who never come near a church should find them marvellous. 'All things were made by God,' says St John, 'and without him was not anything made that was made.'

'All things.' And, therefore, our daily occupations are where we may seek God and find him. Housewife, shop assistant, civil servant, student, 'bus driver, road sweeper, artist, scientist, priest; wherever we work, at whatever we work, whether we are 'in employment' or not – all of us have the self-giving God of the cross at the heart of our very being, and at the heart of our capacities.

A friend of mine, a young priest and singer, used to ask me to accompany him on the piano when he rehearsed before public occasions. Once, he was to sing in the same Holy Week the bass solos in Haydn's *Creation* and the part of Christ in Bach's *St John Passion*. After we had rehearsed the *St John Passion*, ending with the three awesome words of Christ, 'It is finished' – completed – we went on to the *Creation*, beginning with those equally awesome words, 'In the beginning, God created the heavens and the earth.' It's a phrase which requires the singer to imagine, and to enable his listeners to imagine, something like the Michelangelo moment of creation, when the finger of God brings the world and man to life. But to get to the heart of both these phrases, you have to enter into the heart of the same God. Creation and redemption are both achieved by the God whose heart is the cross.

To proclaim that there is a cross in God before ever the wood was seen on Calvary, and that all life is from that tremendous cross hid in the heart of God's love and life, raises many and huge problems. But, for the moment, let us set those problems aside, and spend some time in silence, recollecting the life we know, the life that is familiar to us, and seeing it all within the realm of God's creative cross-like love.

Let us see all that life has handed to us as a gift from the God who is love, and who in his love is our creator, our maker, redeemer and friend. Let us see our life; our friendships, our family life, our life in work or out of it; the politics and people of our country and of our world, from the cross in the heart of God's love and life.

7

Good Friday 2: Entering into the Cross

I put before you in the first address the thought that 'all life is from the tremendous cross hid in the heart of God's love and life'. 'All things were made by God, and without him was not anything made that was made.' But I said that to think in this manner raises many huge problems.

It is, for instance, in some ways fairly easy for at least some of us to believe that all life is from the cross, as we meet here, in the centre of London. We have many of the blessings of nature and civilization to hand. If we cannot believe in God's love here, where will we be able to believe in it? But what about, say, India, where so many babies die before reaching their first birthday; and four out of every ten children die before they are five, and only half the children live to the age of twenty; and most people still suffer from some kind of malnutrition?

If our faith in God – in the cross – is to have deep and lasting value for anyone, it must be able to have such value for all. It's no good our having a kind of Western cross, which will only do for people like ourselves, for our own neighbourhood, and country and generation. Christ's cross is not triumphant – is not therefore the cross – if it has no message, if it cannot avail, if it cannot speak powerfully to all people, of all time, throughout the wide world.

But the stubborn fact is that very many people in this world did not ask to be born, yet poverty and disease are the seemingly unalterable facts of their life. There's little likelihood that in their lifetime they will ever hear about Christ. Many will have no possibility of knowing what we call 'the consolation of his sufferings' with us. They have been 'born to misery as the sparks fly upward'. I think it's these 'facts of life' that make it so difficult for many people to believe in the gospel these days.

But such facts are not really new. It's not simply the sin of man which has caused the problem of world hunger, and its sufferings. Indeed, it's the achievements of modern man that have made possible the relief of much of that suffering.

So, if we sit down before the cross, and say, 'All life is from the cross hid in the heart of God's love and life', we need to hear, surely, an infant voice from, say, Somalia – one of the infants who has survived but may not survive for long – saying, 'Do you mean my life?' And if that country is too remote from our own circumstances to be real, let us reflect that, after all that has been done to get the mentally ill cared for in this country, one in seven of the mentally ill – 42,000 people – still have to be cared for permanently in institutions in England. And if some mental illness is attributable to people's sin – their sin, or their parents' sin or society's sin – it is probable that much mental illness and handicap is attributable, as far as one can see, to no human sin.

But I want to say at this point that I do not think that we shall find any hint of an answer of any depth to this kind of question unless we are willing to engage not just in reasoning, in response to facts and figures, but in pondering and reflecting and wrestling at the most profound level of which we are capable. I believe that the church would be more what Christ would have it be if only we would be silent – silent for a very long while, from time to time – and simply be humble before the realities until they sink into our hearts and minds. The kind of confusion and bewilderment that comes from contemplating the truth of our world today, and of ourselves, before the cross, is, I believe, of God.

If we want to get anywhere near understanding the sufferings of the world, we have to be silent and enter into our Lord's silence upon the cross, and enter into his cry from the cross: 'My God, my God, WHY? . . .' That cry is an essential part not only of prayer, but of faith itself. I think we have to be silent, and to understand Christ's cry from within, and thus the cry of others who are bewildered by their suffering or the suffering of those they love. And that is an essential part of the cry from the cross-in-the-heart-of-God.

Charles Wesley wrote a hymn, which you may well know, but which is probably better read than sung, in which he likened our relationship with God to that of Jacob, who wrestled all night with a messenger from God. That hymn, I believe, indicates how it is part of our Christian, and, indeed, human vocation to wrestle with God about the meaning of life, and the meaning of the world, and the meaning of the cross.

That hymn begins:

> Come, O thou Traveller unknown,
>   Whom still I hold, but cannot see;
> My company before is gone,
>   And I am left, alone, with thee;
> With thee all night I mean to stay,
> And wrestle till the break of day.

There, in that verse, is the Christian – you and I, as would-be Christian believers – still hanging on to God, holding on by faith alone, without much company, in the dark, still wrestling with God and trying to make some sense of life.

The speaker in the poem goes on:

> I need not tell thee who I am,
>   My misery or sin declare;
> Thyself hast called me by my name,
>   Look on thy hands and read it there!
> But who, I ask thee, who art thou?
> Tell me thy Name, and tell me now.

He wrestles on, and continues, in agony. Eventually he cries:

> Yield to me now, for I am weak,
>   But confident in self-despair;
> Speak to my heart, in blessings speak,
>   Be conquered by my instant prayer:
> Speak, or thou never hence shalt move,
> And tell me if thy Name is Love.

There is the Christian, looking into the darkness and misery of so much of the world, and saying to God, 'Tell me if – in spite of all this – thy name is Love.' The poem continues for fourteen verses in the original (although there are usually only five in our hymn books now) until, in the very last verse, the writer exclaims:

> 'Tis Love! 'tis Love! thou diedst for me!
>   I hear thy whisper in my heart;
> The morning breaks, the shadows flee,
>   Pure, universal Love thou art:

> To me, to all, thy mercies move;
> Thy nature and thy Name is Love.

After wrestling in the darkness, not just for five minutes, not just for an hour, but through a long period of darkness of soul, the writer becomes sure that Christ has died to reveal his love for him; and if he is sure of that, then he is certain also that Christ would not have died just for him alone:

> To me, to all, thy mercies move;
> Thy nature and thy Name is Love.

But that conviction only comes with wrestling. It's not a conviction that can be arrived at quickly or glibly. And the wrestling may have to be endured again and again. And the darkness may descend again and again, and the bewilderment and the doubt. But I think that from the cross our Lord does give us certain things to lighten our darkness.

There is, first of all, the odd fact to consider that, though this world contains so much misery for so many, the numbers of those who commit suicide are relatively few, and many of those who do are, alas, out of their minds at the time. On the whole, most of us seem to find something to approve of in this world, in spite of everything. And if you look at photographs of, say, the homeless in one of the great cities of the Third World, and if you read accounts even of the most desperate situations in, for instance, the prison camps of the world, you will often be surprised, indeed, astonished by the joy shown in children's faces and between one person and another. From the cross, in the heart of God, a natural grace seems often to be given to us to bear our burdens; a remarkable resilience; a natural power to delight in something of life; an astonishing capacity to endure, and to discover something for which it is worth enduring.

And there's another fact to consider. To those whom God has given the greatest capacity for life and love, he has also given the greatest capacity for suffering. It's the instruments of greatest sensitivity that are the more easily damaged. With our human sensitivity to warmth, we are also the more easily burnt. Water, which gives us life and health and joy, can as easily drown us. God has made us so finely tuned that our breakdown and our destruction are never far away.

And it's not only Christians who have been willing to recognize that rarely do we learn more, receive more, than from suffering. This

is not, of course, true of all, but I have known and know of many who
conceive of the suffering they have endured as the best gift they have
received from life. They have received it, not masochistically, but
from the cross.

I find myself often asking, what kind of a God would it be who left
no sign anywhere in the world or in history – no sign of light in the
darkness to the thousands and thousands in misery. God would not
have been good. God could not have been God, had he not come at
sometime to this world to share the misery of mankind. This alone, I
believe, is sufficient reason for God becoming man, and suffering and
dying as he did, in Christ, to share, in love, the lot of man; literally
having compassion and sympathy and suffering with and alongside us.
It is, to use the title of an important work of theology, *The Justification
of God*.

It helps me, on Good Friday, to call to mind the man Jesus Christ
who through the evolutionary process was a man like other men. It
helps me to consider the man born not in Western civilization, but in
a Palestine village, 2000 years ago, where poverty and misery must
have been among the unalterable facts of life. It helps me to consider
Jesus growing up, not as an infant prodigy, but learning, like other
boys – which means ignorant, like other boys – subject to want,
subject to misunderstanding. It helps me to consider Jesus as a
creature of his own time, enmeshed in the power structures of his
own time. And it was within that web that Jesus was bound, and free;
suffered, and was triumphant in suffering.

It helps me, on Good Friday, to consider Jesus hungering, feeling,
loving, weeping, bereaved, terrified of death; at the mercy of his
disciples' fecklessness and the treachery of his betrayers; dying, a
young man of 33; innocent, yet nailed to a cross like a rat to a barn
door. It helps me to consider Christ praying in the midst of all this,
bewildered in the midst of all this, asking to be delivered from all this:
'Let this cup pass from me.'

The accounts of Gethsemane in the Gospels differ, yet they each
add something worth adding. Consider Christ's prayer: 'Let this cup
pass from me,' but then consider him praying 'If this cup may not pass
from me' – the cup of his own suffering, the cup of the world's
suffering, the sharing of it all – 'if it may not pass from me except I
drink it, thy will be done.' And consider him saying at the last: 'The
cup which my Father has given me' – has shared with me – 'shall I not
drink it?' Eventually, it is all the 'gift of my Father'. He sees through it

all to the tremendous cross hid in the heart of God's love and life.

The simple fact is there's no 'answer' to the world's suffering. Let's not imagine we shall find an answer to it, a solution to the 'problem of pain' in, say, some book or other. There was no answer to Christ's suffering, only some light upon it, sometimes, in the darkness. The light shines in the darkness, and the darkness does not overcome it – in the end. But Jesus needed to cry in the darkness, 'Why, WHY, hast thou forsaken me?'

It sometimes takes a very long while; we have sometimes to wrestle all night until the break of day before we can cry, 'O ye light *and darkness*, bless ye the Lord.'

So let us keep silence now and enter into some of the bewilderment and darkness of many in the world, this very day. Let us pray for them and for ourselves, that we may be given the faith of Christ to enter deeply into the cross in the heart of God, and into the very nature of him whose nature and whose name is Love.

8

Good Friday 3: The God of Love

In our first hour at the cross, we've been thinking of the cross which begins and ends in the heart of God, but which issues forth in creation itself and then, supremely, in Jesus. God decisively declares himself within his creation, subjecting himself to and within its circumstances and its suffering. St Paul speaks of this most clearly in his Epistle to the Philippians.

> Jesus, being in the form of God, thought this not something to be clung to, but made himself of no reputation, and took upon him the form of a slave, and was made in the likeness of men. And, being found in fashion as a man, he humbled himself and became obedient unto death, even the death of the cross (2.6–8).

There, St Paul declares the compass and scope of the love of God. But there's one aspect of God's love which I think every Christian ought to reconsider each Good Friday and that is the relation of God in his love to human sin, not least to our own sin.

For a number of reasons, I believe it's right to consider other things before we consider this. I believe that we must first see how the cross deals with those things in the world which might, at first sight, argue against God being a God of love at all, for it's essential when we come to think of God's dealings with human sin to know that God *is* a God of love. And I believe that God would have us ask ourselves some very simple questions:

'Do I really believe that God loves me?'
'Do I believe that in the depths of my being?'
'Do I believe he will never cease to love me?'

'Do I believe that all the human love I have received in life is but a pale reflection of his love?'

'Do I believe that whatever else fails, God is always true, loving me and all the world?'

'Do I believe that nothing I can ever do to him or to anyone else will ever stop God loving me?'

That belief in God's love always has been and always will be at the very heart of the Christian gospel.

God is always, always, on my side. He is never, never a tyrant. If he demands something of me, it is, in the end, only for my own good. He loves me for my own sake. He wants me to share in his love because I shall only be myself – I shall only be what he meant me to be when in his love he created me – if I am full of his love. I shall only have the joy and fulfilment he always intended me to have, if I am full of his love. Do I believe that?

If, in these hours at the cross, we came to believe in some new height and depth of God's love, that would be marvellous. Sometimes, I think people take it too much for granted that they do believe in the love of God. 'Why otherwise do you think we are here this Good Friday?', they say. But the simple fact is that, deep down, there is something in most Christians that makes them believe that God will only love them if they are good. They think of sin as failure to reach God's standards, like runners failing to reach a tape, and that God says, 'you have not been honest', 'you have not been pure', 'you have not been loving', and therefore in some way he removes his love from them, or will do.

Now it's true that we suffer for our sins. But it's not true that God punishes us for particular misdeeds. He can only ever have one attitude to us: love. He can only be himself to us. He says, 'I made you for love and life and joy.' He may say, as the Button Moulder said to Peer Gynt, 'You were meant to be a shining button on the world's waistcoat, but your loop got broken.' He may look at us with sadness, the sadness of love. But he never ceases to love us into shape. His love never stops, from eternity to eternity. His love goes on, creating, recreating, restoring.

Yet when God sees that we are using the freedom he has given us to hurt and to destroy ourselves and others, he in his love must do something about it. When God sees the hideous ramifications of evil to which we give free play in his world, in his love he is bound to do something. But what?

Well, let us be clear what even God cannot do. He cannot go back
on his purpose of love in creating us. He cannot take away that
freedom he has given us in creation. That would be to admit defeat,
the defeat of love. If our freedom is the gift of love, he cannot
withdraw the gift without withdrawing the love. To turn us into
unthinking robots, or to melt us down, might have saved him pain
and saved others pain, but it would not have been all that love could
do, the best that love could do.

We now, most of us, recognize that capital punishment – taking
away a life – whatever else it is, is defeat. So indeed is life
imprisonment. Our God-given human insight is that, where human
beings are concerned, love must try to find some way of redemption,
of recreation, of restoration. But how?

Is there any way of restoring our vision of what we ourselves were
meant to be? The trouble with sin is that it gets us accustomed to
what we've become, to loss of vision. It inures us to sin. Is there some
way of loving restoration which doesn't simply say, 'Forget it. It really
doesn't matter.' If nothing matters, why be different? Love cannot just
be 'not bothered' about sin. A truly loving father must reveal at some
stage the hurt a son has caused. Is there some way of forgiveness
which is not just 'cheap and easy'?

The amazing fact about the cross is that it does restore our vision of
who we were meant to be. When we 'Behold the Man' we behold the
image of ourselves. The cross reveals the damage evil does, the pain it
causes. The cross reveals the cost of forgiveness, the suffering love of
God. It's impossible to imagine a more profound, and a more
profoundly loving redemption than the cross.

But it takes time, and it takes all the patience of God – and at the
very heart of that word 'patience' is, of course, suffering. The patience
of God manifests itself most clearly on Calvary, but not only on
Calvary. It takes place here and now, and it needs Jesus, and those he
chooses and empowers, to steward this mystery of his love to us and
the mystery of his forgiveness.

The stewards of the mystery of his love and forgiveness are many
and various. I cannot forget a production of *The Tempest* at the Old
Vic many years ago. It wasn't a particularly great production; and, of
all people, Alastair Sim was Prospero. But it was when, in that last
marvellous scene of reconciliation, I heard the godlike priestly
Prospero say to the savage deformed Caliban, 'This thing of darkness I
acknowledge mine,' that I heard not only Shakespeare, not only

Alastair Sim, but a voice from beyond saying something to me about God's acceptance, God's love, God's forgiveness – and not only of me, but of all personified evil, all darkness.

This theme of God's unconditional love – that he will only deal with us lovingly, though we cannot always deal thus with ourselves – is a theme with which playwrights often wrestle. It's very significant, I think, that John Osborne – that erstwhile 'Angry Young Man' – should have written in the 1960s a play about Martin Luther.

At the centre of his play, *Luther*, is a remarkable dialogue on God's love between Luther and his fellow monk, Brother Weinand while, in the sacristy, the anxious Luther prepares to say his first Mass. Brother Weinand enters in a state of suppressed excitement, with the news that Martin's father has turned up, with a couple of dozen friends and a gift for the Chapter, and is having breakfast with the Prior.

'I should have told him not to come,' is Martin's response, though he asks, significantly: 'Is my mother with him?'

Martin's anxiety state is wonderfully portrayed by Osborne. He is 'running all over with sweat . . . like a pig in a butcher's shop'. He's wondering whether he should shave again. He's concerned with his bowel movements, or lack of them. He's obsessed with the sins he's already confessed. Suddenly, he bursts out: 'What have I gained from coming into this sacred Order? Aren't I still the same? I'm still envious. I'm still impatient. I'm still passionate . . . All you teach me in this sacred place is how to doubt.'

Brother Weinand tells Martin: 'It hurts me to watch you like this, sucking up cares like a leech.' Martin begs him to promise he'll stay beside him during the Mass. Brother Weinand assures Martin that nothing will go wrong, and that if he makes any mistakes, 'we'll see to it'. He then asks Martin to kneel down and say, phrase by phrase, the Apostles' Creed. Martin does so, but inserts between the phrases his own interjections: 'I'm a trough, I tell you, and he's swilling about in me all the time . . . All I can feel is God's hatred.'

When they get to 'I believe in the forgiveness of sins,' Brother Weinand asks: 'Do you?' He adds: 'Then remember this. St Bernard says that when we say this in the Apostles' Creed each one must believe that *his* sins are forgiven . . .' Martin's only comment is: 'I wish my bowels would open. I'm blocked up like an old crypt.'

Well, I'd be surprised if most of us were not still to some extent 'blocked up'. Childhood wounds, doctrinal wounds, and so on, have blocked up our view of God's unconditional love. And we can't get very far until we believe deeply that God has accepted us. That alone will open us up. Otherwise we shall go on bartering our deeds for his love. 'Lord,' we shall say, 'you can love me now because I've done this and that.' Or, more likely, we shall say, 'Lord, you *can't* love me because I've done this and that, and failed to do this and that, because the fact is we're never satisfied that we've been able to scrub our souls clean enough for God, or for others, or for ourselves. So we go on for ever trying to prove something to someone, to prove that we are acceptable.

When I was chaplain of Trinity College, Cambridge, after I'd preached in chapel I used sometimes to escape to the rooms of an undergraduate who was specially gifted at frying chips. He was an agnostic, but a man of tremendous sympathy and friendship with, in many ways, the best brain I've ever come across. One Sunday evening I was surprised to find that he wanted to listen to 'Sunday Half-Hour' on the radio. It was from a church near his home in his native Scotland, and the thoughts of home had triumphed over his thoughts on religion. The minister began the broadcast with an unforgettably terrifying voice: 'The first requirement of the righteous God from us is righteousness.' My young friend grabbed a slipper and hurled it at the radio. 'That is why I don't believe in your bloody God,' he shouted. 'If he were my God,' I said, '*I* wouldn't believe in him.'

To me, the first requirement of the righteous God is not my righteousness, but that I should know that he loves me, and will never stop loving me, no matter how unrighteous I am. He loves this world and will never forsake it. His first requirement is that I should know his heart is like the cross itself, and that nothing will prevent him from accepting me.

9

Good Friday 4: The Body of Christ

We have just been receiving again our acceptance from God who is love, love like the cross. If creation itself stems from the cross in the heart of God, if Christ himself issues forth from the cross in the heart of God, then we must say the same of the life of the church itself, to which St Paul gives that most profound of all titles, 'the Body of Christ'. There's no clearer way of speaking of our acceptance by God than to accept as directly as we can that phrase of St Paul: 'You are the Body of Christ and each of you a different part of it.' Supremely, from the cross, Christ draws us to himself. 'I, if I be lifted up, will draw all men unto me.' Supremely, by the cross, he has made us 'accepted in the Beloved', that cross which is eternally in the heart of God. But then, from the cross, Christ says: 'Receive ye one another' – accept one another – 'as I have received you – as I have accepted you.'

'You are accepted. Now become the Accepting Community.' And from the cross, Christ shows his followers how to begin. He says to John, his beloved disciple, 'John, look after Mary.' He says to Mary, his mother: 'Mary, look after John.' He gives the one to the other, from the cross. In my own ministry, one rather quaint quotation has come to mean more to me than any other in helping me to envisage what Christ means his church to be as the accepting community, in helping me to understand the kind of community the God who was in Christ brings to birth. It comes from the strange ascetic monks who followed St Antony into the Egyptian desert in the third century. Here it is:

A certain old man used to say, 'It is right for a man to take up the burden for those who are near to him, whatsoever it may be and, so to speak, to put his own soul in the place of that of his neighbour and to become, if it were possible, a double man; and he must suffer, and weep, and mourn with him, and finally the matter must be accounted by him as if he himself had put on the actual body of his neighbour, and as if he had acquired his countenance and soul, and he must suffer for him as he would for himself. For thus it is written, "We are all one body." '

The phrase 'bear ye one another's burdens' has a much fuller meaning than is generally ascribed to it. That fuller meaning is no less practical than the usual meanings of 'being sympathetic' and 'doing acts of kindness and love'. It is very proper that they should be done. But that is because we ought to see ourselves as 'members one of another'; membra, limbs, of the same body, not just members of the same society. Christians are not members of a club; they are 'members' of the church, which is not a club. Men and women are not members of a club; they are 'members' of humanity, which is not a club.

I want to provide a very practical commentary on this quotation, to help you, if I can, to think of the kind of church, the kind of community of acceptance which Christ through his cross begets. That strange writer says: '. . . the matter must be accounted by us as if we had put on the actual body of our neighbour. . .'

There are certain incidents in ministry which are unforgettable to each of us. I cannot forget one incident when I was a vicar. It became clear that we ought to try and do something for the old people of our neighbourhood, so we opened a club in the large end room of the Victorian vicarage – my predecessor called it 'the lesser ballroom'! The first afternoon it was opened I stood by the open door of the vicarage, rather surprised at the numbers who were turning up. I said casually to an old man with a stick, whom I later came to know as Mr Buckler: 'Goodness, how many more of you!' 'Didn't you expect so many?' replied Mr Buckler, somewhat acidly. 'No,' I said, 'I expected a handful the first day and that we would have to grow slowly.' 'Then you can't know how lonely some of us are,' he rapped out.

'You can't know how lonely some of us are.' Though those words were said to me around 40 years ago, I shall never forget them. But if a church puts on the actual bodies of those who are near to them, the aged neighbours, for instance, many of them living alone – if it 'takes up the burden for those who are near to them', then it *does* know how lonely some people are, and that knowledge spurs it to action.

But perhaps one of the most frequent remarks I hear from the more elderly church members as I visit different parishes in the course of my ministry is: 'I don't know what's become of young people today . . .' But is it too much to think of the church as a place in which the elderly *do* know what's become of the young people today? Through that grace and power that flows from the creating and renewing God, the elderly may put on the actual body of their young neighbours.

When an elderly person asks God if they can understand from within what it's like to put on the body of their teenage neighbours, extraordinary things begin to happen. Certainly, when the church puts on the actual body of the young neighbours of the locality, a new and practical care often results; when the young are given to the old from the cross, and *vice versa*. On the whole, the church is not so bad at looking after some of the more respectable young people; but it's important also to put on the body of the people who are not so respectable, whom you read about, for instance, in the local papers – the people who often end up in court.

And the quotation does not only say we must put on the body of our neighbour. It says we must put our own soul in the place of our neighbour, our own psyche, and we must acquire his or her soul, his or her psyche. When we hear of other people's failings, it's not difficult to judge and to condemn. But when we put on people's bodies and psyches, what a difference that makes; when we receive their temptations not with our bodies, our upbringing, our education, our background, our psychology, our sexuality, but with theirs. It's easy to label people this and that – divorcee, homosexual, drug addict, vandal – and to point the finger of scorn at them, until we put on their actual body and acquire their soul, and become if it were possible a double man and understand them from within. Then we are on our way towards a community of compassion, a community of acceptance.

Some time ago, in the course of my duties as Preacher to Gray's Inn, I was talking to a judge. He had been listening to a sermon I'd preached in which I happened to say that it must be very difficult for the present occupant of Hatfield House, in the diocese of St Albans, to know what it's like to be a black unemployed teenager living in Brixton. The judge was a good, kind, highly intelligent man; but by way of comment on that phrase in my sermon he said to me afterwards, 'Eric, perhaps it would interest you to know that I "put away" nineteen black teenagers this week. The cameras were fixed on them, in a South London market, and they were photographed in the very act of going through people's pockets and shoplifting. I had no compunction whatsoever in sending them down.'

I thought for a few moments before making any comment, and then I said to the judge, 'Would you mind my asking where you sent your son to be educated?' He named a well-known public school and after that a Cambridge College. Then I asked, 'Do you think if those nineteen black teenagers had been brought up in your home, and then had been sent to the school to which you sent your son, that it's likely you would have been sending them down this week?' 'No,' he said quietly, 'probably not.' 'But,' I said, 'to use your own words, you had *no compunction whatsoever* in sending them down.'

Now it was not the guilt-before-the-law of those teenagers I was in any way questioning; it was the phrase 'no compunction whatsoever'. My dictionary defines compunction as 'uneasiness of conscience, remorse tinged with pity'. When you 'become a double man', when you 'put on the actual body of your neighbour and acquire his countenance and soul', it would be very odd indeed if, at the least, *compunction* were not increased; compunction as part of compassion.

And that phrase 'acquire his countenance' has, of course, a special force where race relations are concerned. There are quite a lot of books written these days about white people who've done all they can to look like black people so that they can experience as much as possible what it's like to be a black person in a predominantly white society. But this act of exchange – black with white, white with black – is not something for a few to undertake. It's in some degree for us all to acquire the countenance of our neighbour.

When you first come to that quotation, it's possible rather to rush over the first words. A certain old man used to say, 'It is right for a man to take up the burden for those who are near to him, whatsoever it may be.' But I think really there's the rub – 'whatsoever it may be'. Then it goes on, 'and, so to speak, to put his own soul in the place of that of his neighbour and to become, if it were possible, a double man'. The point is that, of course, it's *not* possible 'to take up the burden ... whatsover it may be'. And it's the clear impossibility of the task which forces us to a more profound understanding of the passage, forces us not simply to envisage a series of demanding, practical, undertakings which somehow we have to attempt, but forces us to see this whole way of exchange in the light of Christ's birth and life and triumphant suffering, and in the light of the creative and redeeming power of God. It is a way of exchange which can only be undertaken through grace.

That great passage, for instance, in St Paul's Epistle to the Philippians, which I referred to earlier, tells us how Christ himself put on the 'actual body of his neighbour' and that that is what lies at the very heart of the incarnation. 'Let your bearing towards one another arise out of your life in Christ Jesus. For though the divine nature was his from the first, yet he did not prize his equality with God but made himself nothing, assuming the nature of a slave; bearing the human likeness, revealed in human shape, he humbled himself, and in obedience accepted even death.'

But St Paul does not just say that Jesus 'put on our humanity' and that we are to put on the actual body of our neighbour; he says, 'put ye on the Lord Jesus'. Become a double man by becoming Christ. See everything and everyone through his eyes. Ask for his eyes. Ask that 'this mind may be in you which was also in Christ Jesus'. That means entering into Christ's prayer and understanding from within – as his arms stretch out on the cross to embrace young and old, rich and poor, white and coloured, the tempted, the fallen, the sick, the bereaved – how he could say, 'Our Father'.

The last words of that quotation say: 'For thus it is written, We are all one body.'

The Body of Christ is for ever on the cross, and for ever radiant with glory. It always has within it the exchange of Mary and John, of John and Mary. Christ gives his own to one another, and our natural belonging to one another becomes a supernatural belonging, a supernaturally inspired way of exchange: 'I live, yet not I but Christ lives in me,' and we become 'very members incorporate in the mystical body of thy Son which is the blessed company of all faithful people'. Our chief temptation is for our faith to fail; and either we envisage a few human works which we know we can manage, or we so spiritualize the passage that we never see any really practical outcome, or we limit the operation simply to a few friends and family, a few 'buddies'. But the 'good works which thou hast prepared for us to walk in' are to enable the growth, the building up, of 'that Holy Fellowship'.

We are all one body. And it is as members of that body that we are now silent before the outstretched Body of Christ.

10

Good Friday 5: Christ the Victim

When we look at Jesus on the cross, there's no doubt at all about one thing: he's a victim, and he's apparently powerless.

Power and powerlessness is a very important subject in our world today and, from the cross, Jesus silently speaks volumes to us on the subject. You can quickly see who the people are in places of power who put him there: Pilate, Annas, Caiaphas, Herod, Judas and the crowd. But Jesus is clearly a victim. In the end, he can't move a finger or a foot. He can thirst, feel pain, cry out. He can do little else but love or hate. And he chooses to love.

And yet here we are, remembering him today. And the power of Pilate, Annas, Caiaphas, Herod, Judas, that looked so dominant and triumphant, is as though it had never been.

In the last years, time and time again, the victims of the world have hit the headlines, but usually not for long or in great detail. It's often the nature of a victim to escape notice, to receive little attention. The headlines most often stay with the powerful. The victims get the headlines for a few brief hours or days. The film *Schindler's List* brought back to the minds of many of us the victims of the Holocaust; but it came and went.

My first real friendship as a boy was with another 13-year-old, Hans Kisch, whose father was a Jew in Vienna but had been carried off to no one knew quite where. In 1938, Hans brought with him to England, and to our local vicarage, two suitcases. They were all his worldly goods. Shortly after, there came to that vicarage Pastor Heinz Helmuth Arnold, from Buchenwald, emaciated and gaunt, his hands still raw from frostbite. But at that time, and for several years more, the world knew little of the millions of victims of the Holocaust. The first victim only arrived in Auschwitz in July 1940.

There were of course many victims of the Second World War from different races. But when, on 6 August 1945, the first atomic bomb was dropped on Hiroshima, and then a second on Nagasaki, a new dimension of power and powerlessness had been reached in the history of humanity, and in the history of inhumanity. We've all seen photographs of the victims of those two dreadful moments that crowned the success of the scientists who had laboured with such skill, on our behalf, at Los Alamos.

Then we were told that the possession of nuclear arms would keep the peace so that there would be only *limited* and *local* wars.

And while we have gone on, and are still going on, spending huge sums on military budgets, the hungry have starved, because what might have been spent on, for instance, agricultural development, has been spent on arms, bought often at events obscenely called 'Arms Fairs'. But on such occasions, as on most occasions, the victims are out of sight and out of mind. There are millions of victims simply of the priorities of our budgets. The news in recent years has had much in it about the powerful connections between the arms industry and trade. When I was visiting a district in Hyderabad in India, with one tap to 1000 people, I wished I could have brought with me those who were just about to order on our behalf some new and costly piece of military equipment, and faced them with the faces of the people there – the victims.

But in our own country there are now, of course, dramatic divisions between the powerful and the powerless. In my last years as Director of the charity Christian Action I was privileged to see much of the inner cities and urban priority areas. As one of the relatively powerful, it was my lot to be involved in the making and presenting of a film for BBC TV in Middlesbrough, a once powerful town. The coal, iron, steel and shipping industries which made it powerful have all collapsed in the last years and Middlesbrough's future now largely depends on the decisions of the powerful, in faraway London. Middlesbrough as a place, and its people, are victims.

This rehearsal and recalling of some of the facts of power and powerlessness is necessary on this Good Friday because there would be a certain pious escapism about concentrating our gaze on him whom our hymns, for instance, call 'Victim Divine' at the expense of the victims whom his divine humanity focuses and represents. And on

that point we should perhaps dwell a little. Those of us who profess
and call ourselves Christians need to realize that we are caught up for
life in the cause of the victim. And whatever else Good Friday is, it's
not a call simply to contemplate the Crucified, isolated from all other
victims. It's a call to contemplate him who represents all other
victims; that is part of his priesthood.

It would be a remarkable and a transforming thing, if all those who
gathered in our churches this Good Friday – all the powerful –
realized they were binding themselves to the cause of the powerless,
the voiceless, the victims.

There's a panel of stained glass in a French cathedral showing
scenes from the parable of the Good Samaritan. It's no surprise to see
a halo over the figure of the Good Samaritan. But the brightest halo in
one of the windows is over the victim left half dead on the Jerusalem
to Jericho road. The windows are thirteenth century and are saying
with St Augustine that man, the first Adam, is the victim on that road
but that a wounded Man – the Second Adam, Christ the Victim – is
the means of our redemption.

You'll remember, in the parable, that though the priest and the
levite *see* the victim, they pass by on the other side. Part of our
redemption comes through seeing and hearing *the* Victim.

On this Good Friday, most of us are here because we know
salvation comes from seeing the Crucified and hearing him. But he
points us to the victims he represents, and says, 'Is it nothing to you,
all ye that pass by?'

The victims of Auschwitz, of Hiroshima and Nagasaki, are a
redemptive warning to all humanity. We need to see and to face these
victims and hear their cry, as persons like ourselves. In the redemptive
economy of God, those victims have a redeeming power for today's
world.

I sometimes used to sit at table in Trinity College, Cambridge,
with Professor Otto Frisch, who helped make that first atomic bomb.
He told me how, on the day the bomb was dropped on Hiroshima,
when his fellow scientists were celebrating their success, he suddenly
found he could not join them. He had heard the voice of the victims,
and was sick at heart. It was a redeeming sickness.

But not only do we need to see in our mind's eye the victims of
war and of our military budgets, we need to hear and see the victims
of our society, the victims of racial prejudice, the victims of our
housing policy.

Ten years after the publication of the report *Faith in the City*, I went to
Gateshead, Newcastle and parts of County Durham under the auspices
of that remarkable organization Church Action on Poverty, and spent all
day with the Roman Catholic Bishop of Hexham and the Anglican
Bishop of Newcastle, wrestling with some of the questions that massive
unemployment has brought to the North East. On the walls of the
church where we met were posted lists of what unemployed people of
the area had said was their personal experience of unemployment:

Lack of self-respect;
Feeling like a second-class citizen;
Lack of control over one's life;
Loss of a sense of identity and belonging;
Isolation;
A life shapeless and without order;
Strained relationships in the home;
Long-term decline in the quality of life;
Loss of hope;
The struggle to manage, week after week;
Inability to replace ordinary household necessities;
Not being able to support the family;
Conflict over money.

The people were there to speak with us of their experiences, and I
found it deeply moving to talk one-to-one with those who had been
unemployed for several years.

I have tried to suggest that as we look at Jesus on the cross, Jesus
the Victim, we see with him the victims of our day and age. You don't
need me to spell out who are the victims in our society. Pascal said,
'Christ will be in agony until the end of the world,' and that is bound
to be so, for while there is one victim of this world, who can imagine
a Christ who is not alongside that victim?

Earlier this week I spoke of how, when I was a student, I went on a
Retreat whose conductor was Father Edward Keble Talbot. He talked
of Christ the Victim, the victim of betrayal, and he said: 'At the worst
time he did the best deed. The same night he was betrayed he took
bread and broke it and gave it. He used the *betrayal* as the means of the
betrayer's redemption.' I did not really understand the meaning of
those words for another 25 years, but I pass them on to you now. We
are not only to contemplate the Victim. We are to contemplate and
emulate what he did. At the worst time he did the best deed. He used

the betrayal that made him a victim as the means of the betrayer's redemption.

So now,
Let us pray for the victims of our world;
Let us commit ourselves to listen and learn from the victims of our world;
Let us commit ourselves again to Christ crucified, the Saving Victim;
Let us commit ourselves to the redemption of those who betray us.

11

Good Friday 6: Hope beyond Death

'Out of the fire of his love, God creates and sustains man and all the world.' That's what we said at the beginning of these three hours. But, of course, that's not the whole truth. The simple fact is that the God who is love – love like the cross – has created us all for death; for a brief life, and for growth – growth towards death – and for death itself and for what lies beyond. So that the whole of our life has the shadow of death cast upon it, in one way or another, if only in the form of that anxiety which is the hallmark of our knowledge of our mortality. Charles Williams wrote that 'Death is an outrage,' which of course it very often is. We need to remind ourselves that Jesus himself was crucified as a 33-year-old young man. It's difficult, at first, ever to think of death as other than an outrage at that age.

But when you think of the alternatives to death – staying alive for ever and ever and never ageing, which means never growing – some of the blessings of death begin to appear. And you at least begin to see what the God who is love was up to in creating us, including his son Jesus, for death.

When you start thinking of death and the God who is love, you are soon on to the blessing - and curse – of time, that raw material out of which the whole of our life is made. This last year of the old millennium we need to see that time is the raw material of all history. But it's a curious and profound mystery. We have various ways of 'clocking up' the seconds, minutes, hours and days, but we rarely reflect on the nature of time. Einstein plumbed some of the depths of time, but he left a lot of them unplumbed. And they're probably best left to the poets rather than to the philosophers, mathematicians and scientists.

In one of his Sonnets, Shakespeare wrote:

> Time will come and take my love away.
> This thought is as a death, which cannot choose
> But weep to have that which it fears to lose.

Shakespeare, of course, knew more about the curse and blessing of time than any of us or, rather, he could articulate that curse and blessing more penetratingly, and more beautifully, than any of us. But the simple fact remains that the God of love, love like the cross, has created us for death; and has created us – unlike other animals – to be conscious that our death, and the death of everyone we love, never lies far off.

A very good American book on bereavement counselling states that 'No one can help anyone else to die who has not faced their own death.' That sentence hit me so powerfully when I first read it that I shared it with a seminar of medical students I was addressing in Cambridge. They didn't like it at all. They wanted to be doctors; but not to help people to die; and at their age they certainly didn't want to face their own death. Doctoring, they said, was preventing death, and helping to escape it, not face it. A few weeks later I was talking to Dr Cicely Saunders, who pioneered the St Christopher's Hospice for the Dying. I asked her what she thought of the American doctor's phrase. 'Well,' she said, 'I find it difficult to face my own death – not because I don't want to, but because it's so abstract. I don't know whether I'm going to have a heart attack, or a car accident, or a tumour on the brain, or a stroke, or what. I think that I have to get used to death *now*, to recognize it in my own life, in my own body *now*. I've had to retire,' she said. 'I didn't want to. I say I'm perfectly all right and I could go on for years. But that is refusing to face my own death. Death is what happens to me, a bit every day. It's written on every relationship. In the world of things, they call it "built-in obsolescence". And the question is whether we can see the love of God behind it or whether we meet it only with bitterness, regret and hatred.'

There's no greater witness to man's true size and stature than the history of his speculation concerning what will happen when he dies. But in fact we are lost for words. Words fail, and we may use innumerable pictures to comfort ourselves: 'The Islands of the Blest', 'Where the Rainbow Ends', and so on.

The Jews did not believe in any real life-after-death until shortly before the coming of Christ. But they had their word pictures too. The dead led a kind of shadowy existence. And then they began to believe in a resurrection, and the pictures began to get more and more complicated. Subdivisions of heaven for this sort of person and that, and subdivisions of hell for that sort of person and this.

And then came Jesus, and the green hill of Calvary, and his triumph over death. What did Jesus teach us about death?

Well, today we have thought much about what Jesus revealed; that in the heart of God is greater love than we can ever conceive. But this is so great a truth that even Christians have rarely been able to grasp it. They have preferred to go on with their picture-making and their complications and their words. Even within the pages of the Bible the simple fact of God's continuing love gets blurred into all sorts of fantastic pictures of the end of the world, and of the divisions and subdivisions of heaven and hell. But by the Middle Ages there seemed no limits to man's ability to obscure the simple truth.

Let us then this Good Friday take hold again of that simple truth of Gods *unimaginable* love, and that he has prepared for us 'such good things as pass our understanding'.

Let us admit frankly and fearlessly that, concerning the details, our knowledge of what happens when we die is small. Words do fail. The human imagination, great as it is, completely fails. But there is no need for us to try and penetrate the unknown. Jesus has told us all we need to know. He has told us by his life that God is love. Isn't that really all we have been saying throughout today? And doesn't this say all we need to know?

One of the greatest English saints, Julian of Norwich, said almost the last word that has to be said when she wrote: 'Wouldst thou learn thy Lord's meaning in this? Learn it well. Love was his meaning. Who showed it thee? Love. What showed he thee? Love. Wherefore showed it he? For love. Hold thou therein and thou shalt learn and know more in the same. But thou shalt never know nor learn therein other thing without end.'

As far as I am concerned you can throw away almost all the hymns on life after death as long as you leave me with those three words *God is love*. Of course, they are not simple words, but the life and death of Jesus tell us all we need to know of the love of God. Our imagining cannot add to that.

And if that is the truth, we have no need to worry. Our loved ones are in more loving hands than ours. We shall be in more loving hands than we have ever known, than we can ever imagine.

I was very privileged to be allowed to write the life of Bishop John

Robinson, who died of a pancreatic tumour in 1983. When he preached his last sermon in Trinity College Chapel, Cambridge, just before he died, he asked me to sit next to him, in case he couldn't finish it. He did finish it, and this was the last paragraph of his last sermon, on 'Learning from Cancer':

> The Christian takes his stand not on optimism but on hope. This is based not on rosy prognosis (from the human point of view mine is bleak) but, as St Paul says, on suffering. For this, he says, trains us to endure, and endurance brings proof that we have stood the test, and this proof is the ground of hope in the God who can bring resurrection out of and through the other side of death. That is why he also says that though we carry death with us in our bodies (all of us) we never cease to be confident. His prayer is that 'always the greatness of Christ shall shine out clearly in my person, whether through my life or through my death. For me life is Christ, and death gain; but what if my living on in the body may serve some good purpose? Which then am I to choose? I cannot tell. I am torn two ways: what I should like' – Paul says more confidently than most of us could – 'is to depart and be with Christ, that is better by far; but for your sake there is greater need for me to stay on in the body.' According to my chronology he lived nearly ten years after writing those words: others would say it was shorter. But how little does it matter. He had passed beyond time and its calculations. He had risen with Christ.

John Robinson asked that at his Memorial Service this passage from *Le Milieu Divin*, by the great Jesuit priest, paleontologist and philosopher Pierre Teilhard de Chardin, should be read:

> It was a joy to me, O God, in the midst of the struggle, to feel that in developing myself, I was increasing the hold that You have upon me; it was a joy to me, too, under the inward thrust of life or amid the favourable play of events, to abandon myself to Your Providence. Now that I have found the joy of utilizing all forms of growth to make You, or to let You, grow in me, grant that I may willingly consent to this last phase of communion, in the course of which I shall possess You by diminishing in You.
>
> After having perceived You as He who is 'a greater myself', grant, when my hour comes, that I may recognize You under the species of each alien or hostile force that seems bent upon destroying or uprooting me. When the signs of age begin to mark my body (and still more when they touch my mind); when the ill that is to diminish me or carry me off strikes from without or is born within me; when the painful moment comes in which I suddenly awaken to the fact that I am ill or growing old; and above all at that last moment when I feel I

am losing hold of myself and am absolutely passive within the hands of the great unknown forces that have formed me; in all those dark moments, O God, grant that I may understand that it is You (provided only my faith is strong enough) who are painfully parting the fibres of my being in order to penetrate to the very marrow of my substance and bear us away with Yourself.

The more deeply and incurably the evil is encrusted in my flesh, the more it will be You that I am harbouring – You as a loving, active principle of purification and detachment. Vouchsafe, therefore, something more precious still than the grace for which all the faithful pray. It is not enough that I shall die while communicating. Teach me to treat my death as an act of communion.

For Jesus, his death was an act of communion. So let us commend to him those we love but see no longer, and those who are bereaved. And let us see whatever lies ahead of us, and those we love, within the compass of that love, and let us say of them and of ourselves with our Lord himself:

Father, into thy hands I commend my spirit.

12

Easter Day

The Easter Alleluias sum up the joy of Easter. Yet at Easter, I think, almost every priest and many lay people are aware of two emotions, indeed two convictions, that contrast but should not conflict. On the one hand Easter is characterized by phrases such as 'This joyful Eastertide'; but there's a second Easter characteristic.

Every priest and preacher is well aware that there will be some who specially come to church at Eastertide bearing with them the memory of a recent bereavement. I can't myself remember an Easter when I did not come to church without someone specially on my mind who had recently been bereaved. And I always feel an obligation to preach at Easter to what we nowadays call this 'double agenda'.

We should never offer easy words of comfort to the bereaved. The Easter Gospel is not a 'quick fix'.

Rolling away the stone, the stone of bereavement, 'huge as it is', begins for me not on Easter morning, but with everything which confirms for me the reality and nature of God's love. We are all of us created for death – by the God of love – who will still have us in his care when this life is over. God, Jesus revealed, has 'prepared for us such good things' – beyond death – 'as pass our understanding'. St Paul said, 'Now we see in a glass, darkly,' even after the resurrection. 'Now we know in part.'

It does not contradict the joy of this 'joyful Eastertide' to recognize the pain of the present. Easter calls for honesty as well as for faith. The cross was triumphant in suffering, over suffering; but the scars are so visible on the body of the victim.

As we look today on those terrible scenes of thousands upon thousands of Kosovan refugees, hungry, homeless and bewildered, it is impossible simply to say, 'This *joyful* Eastertide ...' and ignore our fellow human beings. The text which I am holding on to this

Eastertide is that verse from Hebrews: 'Now we see not yet all things put under him. But we see Jesus crowned with glory and honour, that he, by the grace of God, should taste death for everyone' (2. 8–9).

As Christians we are an Easter people 'now', but there is still a great deal of 'not yet' about life in this world. 'Now we see not yet all things put under him.'

The hymn that I most want to quote at Eastertide, to those who are bereaved and to those who are facing death, is not 'officially' an Easter hymn. It's by the seventeenth-century Puritan Divine, Richard Baxter:

> Christ leads me through no darker rooms
> Than he went through before;
> He that unto God's Kingdom comes
> Must enter by this door.
>
> My knowledge of that life is small,
> The eye of faith is dim;
> But 'tis enough that Christ knows all,
> And I shall be with him.

Let me end this last of my addresses to you this Holy Week and Easter with a St Stephen's reminiscence, which I hope may have something to say to you all this Easter.

Many a time when I was a curate here, and had to visit someone in the Westminster Hospital, I would go to the chapel and sit or kneel before a marvellous painting of the resurrection by the sixteenth-century Italian painter Veronese, and often the power of the resurrection would seem to flood into me from it.

I particularly remember a six-year-old child, Alastair Hetherington, who came into the hospital with leukaemia. His father and mother were unable to be with him, for his father was high up in the Army. Cuthbert Bardsley, Bishop then to the Forces, asked me to visit Alastair. Bishop Cuthbert came and laid hands on him, while I met with several nurses for prayer in the chapel in front of that painting of the resurrection. Alastair, alas, died. It was, I think, my first experience of the death of someone to whom I had become very attached. I bought a small crucifix, so that I would go on remembering him, and it has been on the chest of drawers in my bedroom ever since.

Recently, that painting of the resurrection has been cleaned and restored, and has been placed in the chapel of the new Chelsea and

Westminster Hospital, in the Fulham Road. New details have been revealed in the painting by restoration.

I have preached to you this week not least about the need for the crucifixion and the resurrection to be held together. They are both manifestations of the love of God and of the power of God in Christ. If you go and see that Veronese painting, you will see what I mean. The action of the painting is at night. It's as though the artist wanted us to be fully aware of the darkness that surrounded the resurrection – the darkness that surrounded and followed the crucifixion – in which the love of God was made manifest; the darkness not least of bereavement. It is the power of the love of God in Christ which causes him to rise, effortlessly, from the tomb. The darkness cannot overcome the love of God. So Christ dramatically strides upwards, and his pink cloak, and banner, and accompanying angels, and the radiant aureole around him, all speak of his Easter triumph.

I hope that some of you this Eastertide will try to make your own personal pilgrimage to that hospital chapel, and ask to be filled with resurrection life, and to be a bearer of that life to others; to all who are bereaved, and to all who are cast down by the events in our world at this Eastertide. In that painting of the resurrection we see Jesus crowned with glory and honour, having tasted death for everyone: for you; for me.

> Christ has been raised from the dead. Alleluia!
> The first fruits of those who have died.
> Alleluia! Alleluia! Alleluia!

PART TWO

Sermons on Several Occasions
1998–2000

13

Come and See

St Mary Abbots, Kensington; 18 January 1998

That simple three-word phrase 'Come and see' occurs twice in the Gospel reading for today (John 1. 35–51). Jesus himself says it first, and then the disciple Philip. It's surely a very appropriate phrase to use at this beginning of another Week of Prayer for Christian Unity: 'Come and see.'

Of course, we ought to be able to say to people, concerning the church, the Body of Christ: 'Come and see,' knowing that their response will be what people said of the first Christians: 'How these Christians love one another!' 'What a wonderful unity in the church they reveal!' But, alas, we meet – or, rather, we fail to meet – as Protestants and Catholics, in separate churches; and, on the whole, we're very comfortable in our little subdivisions of churches. And, sometimes, we even shoot at one another. Perhaps we should be thankful at the beginning of this particular Week of Prayer for the progress of the peace talks in Ireland, and for the courage of some of those taking part.

'Come and see' what the response to the Gospel has been in Ireland, and here in London. In my lifetime and ministy I've had certain experiences of Christian unity and disunity which I can't easily forget.

When I was a curate in Westminster, we had the Roman Catholic Westminster Cathedral in our parish; but we weren't then on speaking terms with the Cardinal and the clergy at the Cathedral, among whom was Derek Worlock. And that was mutual. In 40 years that climate has changed very considerably. Thank God, before he died I counted Archbishop Derek Worlock, of Liverpool, a personal friend.

Earlier this month, I took the funeral of a judge from Gray's Inn, where I was Preacher until last March. Sir John Megaw had been proud of being an Ulsterman, and when we had invited Cardinal Hume to come and preach in the Chapel of the Inn, it was not even certain at first that Sir John and his wife would attend. But at Sir John's funeral, I was thankful to be able to recall how at the lunch after that sermon of the Cardinal's, I caught sight of the Cardinal sitting next to Ella, Lady Megaw, and noticed them laughing together, with the judge looking on, delighted at the obvious pleasure his wife and the Cardinal were taking in talking with one another, and in *meeting*. Unity so often begins not in doctrinal talks but in meeting together, having a meal together. Prejudice thrives in the lack of any deeply personal meeting.

In the 1960s, Bishop John Robinson and I took a group of clergy and laity from the diocese of Southwark to the Abbey at Pontigny, in Burgundy. It was the abbey where Thomas à Becket had spent three years in exile in the twelfth century. In 1953 it had become the headquarters of the *Mission de France*, which trained and supported priests to work in districts and areas of life which in contemporary pagan France were almost completely cut off from the church; and many of the Worker Priest Movement regarded Pontigny as their headquarters. The hierarchy of the Catholic Church had its anxieties about the worker priests, to say the least, and the Cardinal for the area, Cardinal Lienart, had been placed – stationed 'on guard', so-to-speak – at Pontigny. When our party arrived, the Cardinal warmly greeted Bishop John, and said immediately: 'You will, I hope, celebrate Mass for us in the morning.' John Robinson could hardly believe his ears, and said: 'You mean, of course, celebrate Mass for the group I've brought with me.' 'No!' replied the Cardinal. 'We want you to celebrate Mass for us all,' which Bishop John, of course, gladly did. It was a revelation to me that the monolithic Roman Catholic Church was not so monolithic as it seemed and, indeed, as it often claimed to be.

I contrast that Cardinal's kind invitation with the outcry there was recently in Ireland when the new Catholic President received holy communion at the altar of the Cathedral of the Church of Ireland in Dublin.

Perhaps I should add that the Abbey at Pontigny is a place of such transcendent beauty and such manifest holiness that you're not altogether surprised that with the simplicity of its Cistercian architecture the place conveys a special grace to those who go there. Beauty in buildings so often transcends our ecclesiastical divisions. Beauty has something to say to us in our search for unity.

When the vote took place on Anglican-Methodist union in July 1969 and the proposal of union was defeated, I must admit I was greatly dismayed. I happened to have to go to India immediately after that meeting of the General Synod. There I was asked to preach at a service of the United Church of North India in its cathedral in Delhi. It was marvellously refreshing to find there that Anglo-Catholic Anglicans from some of our great Anglican Religious Communities – like the Society of St John the Evangelist and the Cambridge Mission to Delhi – had all unanimously joined in union with Methodists, Presbyterians and Congregationalists to form the one United Church of North India. A unity which was deemed impossible at home, in the mother church, was celebrated with joy and gladness in India.

I have never seen any suggestion that the North India Scheme of Unity compromised theological truth.

This week is called the Week of *Prayer* for Christian Unity. And sometimes the impression is given that this week will be a 'success' – whatever that means – if we manage to gather a few special groups of people to pray for unity. I think myself that something more than this is required.

In the Gospel reading for today, Christ says 'Come and see.' And one thing we need to have at the heart of such a week as this is a clear remembrance, a clear vision, of Christ praying for his disciples: 'That they all may be one; as Thou, Father, art in me, and I in thee; that they may be one in us, that the world may believe that thou hast sent me' (John 17.21).

'One – that the world may believe'. That's the second impetus that we need to have in our heart in this week of prayer: the realization that Christ prayed for the unity of his disciples *that the world may believe*. The world will never believe while Christians bicker and scrap with each other.

I purposely mentioned, earlier, the Worker Priest Movement and the *Mission de France*. The work of that Mission went forward under the inspired leadership of the Archbishop of Paris, Cardinal Suhard, from 1940 to 1949; and from Paris his influence spread throughout France. Suhard was in origin a rather typical French parish priest, with his roots in tradition and the land, but he came to realize that the church could no longer wait for people to come *to* her, but must plunge boldly into the heart of the earthly city, not least his great city of Paris. 'That the *world* may believe' was a phrase branded on his heart.

Cardinal Suhard died in May 1949. The last addresses he gave say not only what he believed about the mission of the church in Paris. They say something to us in London today as we reflect, here and now, on unity, 'that the world may believe'. This is what Suhard said at his jubilee celebrations, just before he died:

> To save Paris means two things: to save souls, and to save the city . . .
>
> To save the souls of Paris: that, my brethren, is the first task. It is for that multitude that I shall have to answer on the Day of Judgement. Do you realize, then, the agony I feel? It haunts me, it is a fixed idea which never leaves me. When I go round the suburbs with their dreary factories, or the brightly lit streets of the centre, when I see that mass of people, some refined, some destitute, my heart is torn with pain. And I have not far to seek for the subject of my meditation; it is always the same: there is a wall separating the church from the masses. That wall must be levelled at all costs, to give back to Christ the crowds who have lost him . . .
>
> To save the city, my friends, means first of all to save the souls of its inhabitants. But it also means to save the city, that is, to assume responsibility for it as it is, with its past, its future, and the complex problems of its present. If I leave that aside, if I am not concerned about them, I am failing in half of my mission . . .

In this week of prayer for *unity* we must not forget that unity is that the world, the world of this great city, may believe.

But there is one more concern which must be ours this Week of Prayer for Christian Unity. Christ prayed for his disciples: 'Sanctify them through thy truth: thy word is truth' – consecrate them by the truth. All too often it is the assumption that we have the truth, all of the truth, that is the very cause of much of our Christian disunity.

I want to suggest to you that in our time no poem has been more fruitful for Christians – but not only for Christians – than T. S. Eliot's 'Journey of the Magi', which he wrote 70 years ago. If you need something to help you this week, read again 'Journey of the Magi'. Read it, maybe, with other Christians; read it with those who cannot call themselves Christians, and ask yourself – and them – what this poem has to say about the truth of Christ. What does it have to say about the truth which is greater than any church or any denomination, and yet which confronts us all through our very existence: the mystery of truth, which is not least the mystery of ourselves, and the journey which all of us know is ours, and not just other people's – the journey of discovery which none of us has yet completed.

> 'We returned to our places,' say the Magi,
> 'these Kingdoms,
> But no longer at ease here, in the old dispensation.'

This week:
Come and see a church, seeking unity that the world may believe.
Come and see those who like ourselves are seekers after truth.
Come this Epiphany and see 'this Birth':

> ... this Birth was
> Hard and bitter agony for us.

No week of Prayer for Unity can be without its agony. But it is one more step along the way of truth.

'Come and see.'

14

Other Men's Flowers

St Michael and All Angels, Withyham
28 June 1998

My sermon for you this morning, for better, for worse, will be unlike any sermon you've ever heard before.

One of my very favourite books is *Other Men's Flowers*. Some of you, I'm sure, will know it well. It first appeared in 1944, and is the personal selection of poetry by Field Marshal Lord Wavell. Wavell was one of the most civilized of military men there ever was – though, alas, he was never greatly appreciated by Winston Churchill. He called his collection *Other Men's Flowers* because the seventeenth-century French essayist, Montaigne, had written:

> I have gathered a posie of other men's flowers,
> and nothing but the thread that binds them is my own.

Well, that is what I'd like to offer you this morning by way of a sermon, for your Flower Festival – *Other Men's Flowers*. But first, just a word about flowers and gardens.

When Christians have come to write about them, they have all too often and too quickly turned flowers and gardens into metaphors. So the Roman Catholic writer, Richard Challoner, produced, in 1740, as a prayer book for the laity, *The Garden of the Soul*, which has remained – with good reason – one of the favourite devotional books of English Roman Catholics. I don't think we ought to turn flowers and gardens into metaphors too quickly. We ought first to prize them for themselves, and thank God for them.

There are, of course, a few great poems, like Wordsworth's 'To Daffodils', that are about flowers themselves, but most poems – such as those to roses, for instance – are actually to people. Edmund

Waller's 'Go, lovely rose' and Robert Herrick's 'Go, happy rose', of the same period, are examples. So I would want to start my *Other Men's Flowers* with Shakespeare. There are few more beautiful passages in all Shakespeare than just four lines in *A Midsummer Night's Dream*, when Oberon addresses Puck:

> I know a bank whereon the wild thyme blows,
> Where oxslips and the nodding violet grows:
> Quite over-canopied with lush woodbine,
> With sweet musk roses and with eglantine.

Such lines can make us thankful for glimpses of God in wild flowers as well as in garden flowers and gardens.

I want to go next to George Herbert who, after Westminster School, went up to Trinity College, Cambridge, where I was chaplain three and a half centuries later. His classical scholarship and musical ability – he played the lute and viol and sang – secured him a Fellowship at Trinity in 1614. His success seemed to mark him out for the life of a courtier. The death of James I and the influence of his friend Nicholas Ferrar of Little Gidding led him, however, to ordination in 1630 and to the little parish of Bemerton, just outside Salisbury, where he died in 1633, only 40 years old. Before he died, Herbert entrusted his poems to Nicholas Ferrar. One called 'The Flower' reveals the profound experience both of religion and life that had been Herbert's in his brief life.

> How fresh, O Lord, how sweet and clean
> Are thy returns! ev'n as the flowers in spring;
> To which, besides their own demean,
> The late-past frosts tributes of pleasure bring.
> > Grief melts away
> > Like snow in May,
> As if there were no such cold thing.
>
> Who would have thought my shrivelled heart
> Could have recovered greennesse? It was gone
> Quite under ground; as flowers depart
> To see their mother-root, when they have blown;
> > Where they together
> > All the hard weather,
> Dead to the world, keep house unknown.
>
> These are thy wonders, Lord of power,
> Killing and quickning, bringing down to hell

And up to heaven in an hour;
Making a chiming of a passing bell.
    We say amiss,
    This or that is:
Thy word is all, if we could spell.

O that I once past changing were,
Fast in thy Paradise, where no flower can wither!
Many a spring I shoot up fair,
Offring at heav'n, growing and groaning thither:
    Nor doth my flower
    Want a spring-shower,
My sins and I joining together.

But while I grow in a straight line,
Still upwards bent, as if heav'n were mine own,
Thy anger comes, and I decline:
What frost to that? what pole is not the zone,
    Where all things burn,
    When thou dost turn,
And the least frown of thine is shown?

And now in age I bud again,
After so many deaths I live and write;
I once more smell the dew and rain,
And relish versing: O my only light,
    It cannot be
    That I am he
On whom thy tempests fell all night.

These are thy wonders, Lord of love,
To make us see we are but flowers that glide:
Which when we once can find and prove,
Thou hast a garden for us, where to bide.
    Who would be more,
    Swelling through store,
Forfeit their Paradise by their pride.

And then, another hymn-writer, Isaac Watts, born 40 years after George Herbert. Herbert was, of course, the epitome of the Church of England. Watts was a nonconformist, born in Southampton. He went to the Dissenting Academy in Stoke Newington, and became the pastor of the Independent Congregation in Mark Lane, in the City. His health deteriorated, and in 1712 he resigned, and spent the rest of his life in Stoke Newington. Watts wrote many hymns that are favourites still, among them 'When I survey the wondrous cross', and deservedly merits a high place among hymn-writers. But one of his loveliest poems is less well known; and I shall want it among my *Other Men's Flowers*:

> Christ hath a garden walled around,
> A paradise of fruitful ground,
> Chosen by love and fenced by grace
> From out the world's wild wilderness.
>
> Like trees of spice his servants stand,
> There planted by his mighty hand;
> By Eden's gracious streams, that flow
> To feed their beauty where they grow.
>
> Awake, O wind of heaven, and bear
> Their sweetest perfume through the air:
> Stir up, O south, the boughs that bloom
> Till the beloved Master come:
>
> That he may come, and linger yet
> Among the trees that he hath set;
> That he may evermore be seen
> To walk amid the springing green.

Willam Blake, a contemporary of Watts, was by profession an engraver. His poems are often obscure in their imagery. He experienced the darker side of life as well as the sense of the divine dwelling in everyone, in 'Mercy, Pity, Peace and Love'. Blake became opposed to dogma and asceticism. His visionary genius, both as poet and artist, has been increasingly admired. I'd want his poem 'The Garden of Love' in my collection, because it says something that most of us need to hear:

> I went to the Garden of Love,
> And saw what I never had seen:
> A chapel was built in the midst,
> Where I used to play on the green.
>
> And the gates of this chapel were shut,
> And 'Thou shalt not' writ over the door;
> So I turned to the Garden of Love
> That so many sweet flowers bore;
>
> And I saw it was filled with graves,
> And tomb-stones where flowers should be;

And priests in black gowns were walking their rounds,
And binding with briars my joys and desires.

I'd simply love to have something of Housman in my posie of
Other Men's Flowers. And I've no doubt what it should be. We most
of us go on remembering A. E. Housman, not primarily because of
the several volumes of his edition of *Manilius*, to which he
consecrated most of his energies for 40 years. We remember him
because he composed some of the most exquisite lines in the whole
treasury of English verse.

When I was chaplain of Trinity College, Cambridge, I occupied
rooms in Whewell's Court, where Housman was still a legend. There
was an avenue of cherry trees that had been planted on the Backs to
Housman's memory. So, for all sorts of reasons, this poem of his
would find a place in my collection:

> Loveliest of trees, the cherry now
> Is hung with bloom along the bough,
> And stands about the woodland ride
> Wearing white for Eastertide.
>
> Now, of my threescore years and ten,
> Twenty will not come again,
> And take from seventy springs a score,
> It only leaves me fifty more.
>
> And since to look at things in bloom
> Fifty springs are little room,
> About the woodlands I will go
> To see the cherry hung with snow.

Because I went from Trinity to be Warden of the Trinity College
Mission in Camberwell, in South London, I have had reason to go
back to Trinity many times. One day when I went back I was told that
the avenue of cherries was in full bloom and was looking its very best.
I thought I'd wait till the morning to visit it. But that night there was a
heavy frost, and the 'white for Eastertide' turned black. I felt very
angry, with the anger of bereavement, until I reminded myself that on
this planet death is in all that is natural. 'The grass withereth; the
flower fadeth.' 'Now we know in part.' We shall only know Easter in
its fullness in another world than this.

Wavell's *Other Men's Flowers* is over 400 pages long. I daren't detain
you many minutes more, but I must include in my selection for your

Flower – and therefore, Garden – Festival, one poem of Rudyard
Kipling's. Kipling is such an underestimated poet, especially by those
who, because he wrote in the days of Britain's empire, condemn his
patriotism as jingoism and ignore not only the great body of his work
which is far removed from that sphere, but also his own trenchant
criticism of aspects of colonialism. Kipling, it should not be forgotten,
won the Nobel Prize for Literature in 1907. Great poetry can often be
deceptively simple.

Kipling wrote this magnificent poem, 'The Glory of the Garden',
for C. R. L. Fletcher's *A History of England* in 1911.

> Our England is a garden that is full of stately views,
> Of borders, beds and shrubberies and lawns and avenues,
> With statues on the terraces and peacocks strutting by;
> But the Glory of the Garden lies in more than meets the eye.
>
> For where the old thick laurels grow, along the thin red wall,
> You find the tool- and potting-sheds which are the heart of all;
> The cold-frames and the hot-houses, the dungpits and the tanks,
> The rollers, carts and drain-pipes, with the barrows and the planks.
>
> And there you'll see the gardeners, the men and 'prentice boys
> Told off to do as they are bid and do it without noise;
> For, except when seeds are planted and we shout to scare the birds,
> The Glory of the Garden it abideth not in words.
>
> And some can pot begonias and some can bud a rose,
> And some are hardly fit to trust with anything that grows;
> But they can roll and trim the lawns and sift the sand and loam
> For the Glory of the Garden occupieth all who come.
>
> Our England is a garden, and such gardens are not made
> By singing: 'Oh, how beautiful!' and sitting in the shade,
> While better men than we go out and start their working lives
> At grubbing weeds from gravel-paths with broken dinner-knives.
>
> There's not a pair of legs so thin, there's not a head so thick,
> There's not a hand so weak and white, nor yet a heart so sick,
> But it can find some needful job that's crying to be done,
> For the Glory of the Garden glorifieth every one.
>
> Then seek your job with thankfulness and work till further orders,
> If it's only netting strawberries or killing slugs on borders;
> And when your back stops aching and your hands begin to harden,
> You will find yourself a partner in the Glory of the Garden.

Oh, Adam was a gardener, and God who made him sees
That half a proper gardener's work is done upon his knees.
So when your work is finished, you can wash your hands and pray
For the Glory of the Garden, that it may not pass away!
And the Glory of the Garden it shall never pass away!

I must tell you that, while I was preparing my sermon, in my study, which overlooks the garden which is in the middle of our crescent of houses in Kennington, from the window I could see several of the young people – most of them disadvantaged, mentally, and sometimes physically – who are being trained as gardeners by a splendid local Lambeth charity called Roots and Shoots. They were budding the roses, and clearing the weeds from the flower beds and from between the flagstones. It was, in fact, they who reminded me of Kipling's poem.

Kipling was writing nearly 90 years ago, at a time when unskilled labourers did a lot of the work of the world which is now done by machines. But, I suspect – indeed, I believe – we should be employing a good many who for one reason or another will never be capable of great academic success to care for the environment and, indeed, for people. The idea of our country as a 'garden' in which there's a job for everyone to do, some will regard nowadays as romantic; but I think Kipling's vision has much to offer still.

And I hope that at your Festival you will spare a thought for those who might be gardeners if only they were trained for employment; for the young 'roots and shoots' of our society who might be gardeners. It's a charity which I commend to you for your support: Roots and Shoots. To repeat those wonderful lines of Kipling:

There's not a pair of legs so thin, there's not a head so thick,
There's not a hand so weak and white, nor yet a heart so sick,
But it can find some needful job that's crying to be done,
For the Glory of the Garden glorifieth every one.

For the glory of the garden, let us give Glory to the Father, and to the Son, and to the Holy Spirit. Amen.

15

Christic the Entertainer

St Nicholas, Brighton; 27 September 1998

Tuesday is Michaelmas Day – the Feast of St Michael and All Angels – so I take as my text: 'Be not forgetful to entertain strangers, for thereby some have entertained angels unawares' (Heb. 13.2). I suspect that here at St Nicholas, Brighton, you are not entirely unused to entertaining strangers, and yet I'd be surprised if you put entertainment near to the very heart of the Gospel. And the purpose of my sermon this morning is simple. It's to persuade you to do just that: to put entertainment near to the heart of the Gospel.

To begin, perhaps you'll allow me to go to the Oxford Dictionary for a definition. 'To entertain', it says, comes from the Latin *intertenere*: to hold mutually; to occupy for a specific time; to engage the attention agreeably; to amuse; to receive as a guest; to admit to consideration; to cherish; to encounter.

Then I should like to go to the Dictionary of Quotations. But beside my text 'Be not forgetful to entertain strangers' I want you only to take note, at the moment, of but one quotation, and that quotation requires that I should give you the whole poem in which it's set. The poem will be familiar to some of you, I suspect. It's in a Christ Church, Oxford, manuscript that's several centuries old and is sometimes simply called *Preparations*.

> Yet, if His Majesty, our sovereign Lord,
> Should, of his own accord,
> Friendly himself invite,
> And say, 'I'll be your guest tomorrow night',
> How would we stir ourselves, call and command
> All hands to work! Let no man idle stand!
>
> 'Set me fine Spanish tables in the hall;

See they be fitted all;
And there be room to eat,
And order taken that there want no meat,
See every sconce and candlestick made bright,
That without tapers they may give a light.

Look to the presence: are the carpets spread,
The dazie o'er head,
The cushions in the chairs,
And all the candles lighted on the stairs?
Perfume the chambers, and in any case
Let each man give attendance in his place.'

Thus, if a king were coming, would we do;
And 'twere good reason too;
For 'tis a duteous thing
To show all honour to an earthly king,
And after all our travail and our cost,
So he be pleased, to think no labour lost.

But at the coming of the king of Heaven
All's set at six and seven;
We wallow in our sin,
Christ cannot find a chamber in the inn,
We entertain him always like a stranger,
And, as at first, still lodge him in the manger.

That poem – and those last two lines in particular – speak to us of all
sorts of aspects of our life:

The preparations for the liturgy;
The preparations for other church occasions;
The provision of hearing aids and sound systems that work;
Making the church look beautiful;
Preparing the music and the readings and the prayers;
Providing things that make people feel welcome, and that enable
    people to follow the service more easily;
Concern for language that is both beautiful and ministers to
    understanding;
Aids for different age groups and the disabled.

And all this involves expenditure in various ways.

But our work is, of course, not confined within the church
building. That poem speaks of how we look after people when they
phone us, and when they come to our home. How we listen to them.

How we, all of us, get trained to be of real help to them, and how we train others for ministry to Christ in others. 'We entertain him like a stranger.' A lot of 'Christian action' is there – or the want of it – in race relations, and relations that transcend class and sexuality.

I recommend that this week you simply read through slowly one Gospel – say, St Luke's Gospel – and see what each chapter, indeed, each verse, has to say about entertaining; or, rather, see what it has to say about Christ the Entertainer.

Let me give you just an example or two. If, for instance, the Beatitudes reflect something of the original form of what Jesus himself said, what do they say about giving people memorable and beautiful teaching? Teaching – and preaching – as entertainment? As what gives delight as well as truth and challenge?

Then there's the Feeding of the Five Thousand. Or take the passage in Luke 7 in which Jesus is invited to a meal at a Pharisee's house, and a woman with an immoral reputation anoints his feet with her tears and wipes them with her hair. How does Jesus receive her, entertain her? Does he remark on the ointment, and wonder where she got the money to pay for it, or how she earned it?

> He turned to the woman and said unto Simon, 'Seest thou this woman? I entered into thine house, thou gavest me no water for my feet; but she hath washed my feet with her tears, and wiped them with the hairs of her head ... Her sins, which are many, are forgiven, for she loved much.'

Or think on that saying: 'Suffer the little children to come unto me ...' He entertains them. Or on Zaccheus. Jesus says, 'I want to have a meal with you.' Often we entertain by accepting an invitation. Or think about the story in Luke 16 about the rich man who feasted sumptuously every day and Lazarus who would have been glad to satisfy his hunger with the scraps from the rich man's table. What does that parable of entertainment have to say?

But there is material not only in the Gospels. In the Epistles you will find the repeated phrase 'given to hospitality' and St Paul's marvellous words: 'Receive ye one another as Christ received you, to the glory of God the Father.'

But if you do simply read through a Gospel, I'm sure of one thing: that when you come to the institution of the eucharist, to the first Last Supper, there you will see its meaning afresh if you say, here is Christ the Entertainer who takes bread, and gives thanks, and breaks it and gives it to his disciples – people like you and me – and says, 'This is my body which is given for you.'

So I set before you today the theme of Christ the Entertainer; but that is not the whole theme. Within it there is also an invitation. Entertain one another as Christ entertained you.

I will dare to say that Christ was priest, pastor and prophet in his entertaining, in whom he entertained and how he entertained them. Go and do thou likewise. And remember: 'Be not forgetful to entertain strangers' – as Christ entertained strangers – 'for thereby some have entertained angels unawares.' There's no theme closer to Christ's heart – of which I should remind you, as you prepare for Michaelmas – than Christ the Entertainer.

16

St Francis and Harvest

Trinity Methodist Church, Plumstead
4 October 1998

I am delighted to be with you for your Harvest Festival today. Until I was six or seven, I attended the Methodist church – where I was brought up – in Chadwell Heath, north of Dagenham, across the river. I only became an Anglican because our Methodist church, of corrugated iron, closed down. But I received a rich harvest from that church and its Sunday school which I still draw upon.

Another reason for my delight and joy at being here today is that St Francis is a favourite saint of many; but for several years, I was what was called an 'oblate' of the Franciscans, which means you're on the first rung of the ladder to becoming a Franciscan. So 4 October – the Feast of St Francis – has always been important to me. It happens also to be the anniversary of my first celebration of holy communion, 46 years ago, when I was a curate at St Stephen's, Rochester Row, in Westminster. So there are a harvest of things I want to celebrate with you this morning at your Harvest Thanksgiving. And I thought I'd talk to you, rather than preach to you, about what I think St Francis has to say to us at a Harvest Festival.

First of all, let me remind you that for 23 years, Francis was simply the son of a very well-to-do father, in Italy, nearly 800 years ago. In his late teens and early twenties, he was a sort of ne'er-do-well, a tearaway. He was living it up, in every sort of way. He was a reprobate, a lout and a layabout. And then one day he saw a leper in the street; and instead of backing away from him, he kissed him. And after that, he immediately embraced a life of poverty. The verse from chapter 10 of St Matthew's Gospel, 'Take no gold or silver or copper with you', Francis took literally.

Let's stop there for a moment, and think about what that bit of the life of St Francis may have to say to us today.

Very rarely do conversions happen in a split second. They may *appear* to, on the surface. I can't myself believe that Francis had given no thought whatever to his future, or to his past; to what a waste of his gifts his present way of life was. It's more than likely that he'd thought, however fleetingly, of the harvest of his gifts; what it was and what it might have been, and what it might yet be. His conversion, that seems to be all of a sudden, almost certainly signifies quite a period of knowing he was getting nowhere, that this wasn't what his life was meant to be.

Francis speaks to us all of the better life we all know in our deep heart's core we have it in us to live. But it took a crisis for Francis' life to change, a crisis and a decision. The decision was enshrined in that memorable move of Francis to kiss the leper. Crises in our lives often look negative at the time, but within them are concealed gifts. Francis always had had this capacity for compassion, but now he let it come to the top surface. And, immediately, he embraced a life of poverty.

Poverty is rarely good in itself. Indeed, we're all well aware that poverty can be evil. Francis didn't do things by halves. He knew he was called – called by God – to embrace a life of poverty. What does that say to us at Harvest Festival?

I think that first it reminds us that God calls us all. We all have a vocation, a call from God, and that call has something to say to us about how we relate to those who are less fortunate than ourselves: how we relate to the poor and to the hungry, and not only in this country.

For Francis it meant a life of poverty. For the rest of us – most of us – it means learning something which it takes a lifetime to learn, to acquire. It means that we seek the virtue of detachment, of never being possessed by the things we possess or might possess.

All Christians have a vocation to *detachment*, as followers of Christ. Some, relatively few, like St Francis, have a special vocation to poverty itself. Not having his vocation doesn't let us off the hook. We are all called to detachment, detachment from things and people. And that's not easily or quickly learned.

> All good gifts around us
> Are sent from heaven above

we sing at Harvest. And Harvest, I believe, should renew in us a sense that all our possessions are gifts entrusted to us by God, but only for a time, whether they be things or persons. That sense that God has entrusted to us things and people – for a time – should be at the very heart of the Christian life, not just at the heart of Harvest, and Harvest Festival. It's that detachment which will free us to share what we have with others.

Francis was soon aware that he couldn't manage his vocation by himself. But he said: 'God sent me brothers.' Many of us today learn about St Francis from the Franciscans. But it wasn't only Francis who couldn't manage by himself. We all need our fellow Christians, and they need us.

The fellowship of fellow Christians is hugely important to the Christian life. It's part of the harvest; of friendship; of working together in the world to transform it, so that it may the more reveal the kingdom of God on this earth. Playing our part in the fellowship is of huge importance, as 'fellow-labourers' in the harvest. 'God sent me brothers,' said St Francis. And God also sent him Clare and the Poor Clares. God sent him sisters as well as brothers. And he sent us all brothers and sisters in Christ, as part of the harvest of life.

But the fellowship of Christians is not only a fellowship of *good* things. There are always 'tares among the wheat'. We are all of us corrupt as well as godly. So the church is nearly as in need of redemption as the world.

St Francis was devoted to Christ within the church and over against the church. He was sent to reform the church. He was sent to the world and the church, when the church was growing cold. He was sent to inflame it with the love of God; to be a light in the darkness, to be a beacon.

But as a reformer of and in the church, Francis never ceased to be a man of joy. Joy was one of his greatest gifts. And I think that joy which Francis felt was the harvest of a thankful heart and of a heart that was centred in prayer, the prayer of thanksgiving. The friends and followers of Francis often came upon him rapt in prayer on the mountainside. We learn from his disciples that his prayer often consisted of two simple but profound questions: 'What art thou, dearest Lord? and who am I?'

Whenever our prayer is dry and seems fruitless; whenever it seems to be getting nowhere, bearing no harvest, it's aways worth returning to those two simple prayers of St Francis: 'What art thou, dearest Lord? and who am I?'

On one occasion, we're told, his disciples crept up on St Francis when he was deep in prayer, and they were astonished to see the wounds of Christ on his hands and feet – the Stigmata, as we call them. Psychology these days has its comments to make on such manifestations, comments that are often fairly cynical. I think it's right that psychology should be encouraged to comment on such experiences, but should not be allowed to have the last word.

Cardinal Newman wrote: 'Learn that the Flame of Everlasting Love doth burn ere it transform.' The Stigmata of St Francis could well be the fruit, the harvest of St Francis' profound mystical experience of the Everlasting Love revealed in the crucified Jesus.

There's a last thought I'd like to leave with you at your Harvest Festival, a last thought on St Francis. We shall soon be singing the hymn of St Francis, 'All creatures of our God and King', which is based on his Canticle of the Sun. There's a wonderful Harvest thought:

> All creatures of our God and King,
> Lift up your voice and with us sing
> Alleluia, alleluia!

It goes through verse by verse, spelling out many of God's creations: sun, moon, wind, clouds, daybreak, evening, water, fire, flowers, human beings – seven verses in all. It tells us how Francis called every creature his brother or sister. That's where his love of animals was rooted. And that's where his love of human beings was rooted, and his proper love and reverence for all created things. And his prayer for peace begins with this reverence for life and with his poverty. Without possessions it is not necessary to be so keen on defence.

The penultimate verse speaks of death as part of God's gifts of the harvest. That's both a tough and a profound thought. Our life itself has a harvest. The harvest of each one of us is different: of works good and bad; of relationships, physical and spiritual; of the children we produce, and the God-children, and the friendships. But we know that life is brief, and that the most certain fact of life is death. We can either treat death as the enemy, or we can learn to treat it as a friend.

No one has taught us better to treat death as a friend than St Francis:

> And thou, most kind and gentle death,
> Waiting to hush our latest breath,
>   O praise him, alleluia!
> Thou leadest home the child of God,
> And Christ our Lord the way hath trod;
>   O praise him, O praise him,
>   Alleluia, alleluia, alleluia!

Well, death isn't always gentle. For some, alas, it is painful and slow; for others it is sudden and violent. Yet, to the Christian, the heart of what St Francis says is true: that death leads us home to God 'the way that Christ our Lord hath trod'. No death was more violent than his, and if our death is violent we have Christ for a companion. But whatever kind of death is ours, it leads the child of God home to the Everlasting Love. And our Father gathers us into his Harvest Home.

When I was ordained in 1951 I received a telegram from one elderly blind lady which simply said: 'Harvest Home: alleluia!' But I was only 26 then! But when I die – and when you die – that will be the message that should be sent to our friends: 'Harvest Home: alleluia!'

Thank you for letting me share with you these thoughts on St Francis and the harvest. Let me end with the prayer for this Feast of St Francis:

> O Lord Jesus Christ, Who, when the world was growing cold,
> to inflame our hearts with the fire of Thy love,
> renewed in the body of St Francis
> the marks of thy Passion,
> Grant that following his example
> we may bear the Cross
> in the world today
> Till we come to thine Everlasting Kingdom.
> Through Jesus Christ our Lord. Amen.

17

St Luke's-tide Service

St Bartholomew's and the Royal London School of Medicine and Dentistry at the Priory Church of St Bartholomew the Great; 20 October 1998

> 'Only Luke is with me.'
> II Tim. 4.11
> 'Luke, the beloved physician.'
> Col. 4.14

Those two texts together have always seemed to me a poignant and powerful sign and symbol of the human relationship, the human dimension, which lies at the very heart of the medical profession. 'Only Luke is with me' ... 'Luke, the beloved physician'. As someone who has served now not far short of 50 years in the ordained ministry, I want to reflect with you today on that human relationship, that human dimension, with its more than human significance. And I want to speak from my own personal experience.

I begin with my memory as a child of our family doctor. Dr Frew, a Scot, and a sort of Dr Cameron, was a friend of and to our family, and not only to our family. He brought me into the world, but I remember him first, and particularly, on 7 October 1930. Although I was only five and a half, I can date it so precisely because that day the airship R101 flew over our house on its last and tragic journey to Beauvais, where it crashed. I was in bed with diphtheria, but when I heard excited voices in our back garden, I got out of bed to see the airship; but then I heard my mother anxiously calling me to 'get back into bed at once'. Dr Frew, she said, had just summoned the ambulance to take me to the fever hospital. In minutes, it came. I remember the ambulance men carrying me downstairs, wrapped in a scarlet blanket. Dr Frew stood at the foot of the stairs as I was carried out.

'Only Luke is with me' . . . 'Luke, the beloved physician'.

Ten years later, in 1940, during the Second World War, a land mine was dropped on Chadwell Heath, among other high explosives. Dr Frew was at the heart of the care for those who had been killed or injured or bereaved. Perhaps you can understand why 'Only Luke is with me' . . . 'Luke, the beloved physician' has always meant so much to me.

It was more than another ten years before I was ordained. When I was a theological student at King's College, London, living in Westminster, Dr Geoffrey Hale, having a practice in Pimlico, had begun to look after me. When, the first year after my ordination, it was clear that I had contracted tuberculosis, Dr Hale was very helpful in seeing that I went away for a while, to a sanatorium at Eastbourne. I could go on to speak of other GPs who have looked after me, in Cambridge and Camberwell, in St Albans and Kennington.

Now that I am well over three score years and ten, I regard Dr David Poole, at the Hurley Clinic in Kennington, as one of my closest and most valued friends. There are at least half a dozen doctors at the Hurley Clinic, yet I think the personal relationship between the doctors and their patients is no less there than what it was between Dr Frew and my family.

'Only Luke is with me' . . . 'Luke, the beloved physician'.

When I was ordained to a curacy in Westminster, there were five hospitals in the parish; the Westminster, the Westminster Hospital for Children, the Grosvenor Hospital, the Gordon Hospital and the British Empire Nursing Home. None of them are there today. From the beginning of my time in the parish, I had 40 beds to visit each week in the Gordon Hospital and, at least once a week, a story to tell to a ward full of children in the Westminster Children's Hospital. But there was always someone to visit in the Westminster Hospital itself, and nurses, doctors and medical students were a significant part of our congregation. One of the St Thomas's nurses' homes was in the parish.

I left Westminster to be chaplain of Trinity College, Cambridge, and found myself caring for many medical students, some of whom came on from Cambridge to this very place. Many of the medical students I knew at Cambridge have remained friends for life, and have helped me to go on thinking about the continuously changing medical scene. Amidst all that rapid and radical change, it has seemed to me important to hold to the human relationship and the human dimension at the very heart of the medical profession.

'Only Luke is with me' ... 'Luke, the beloved physician'.

In the course of my ministry I have been privileged to have seen something of the work of all the major London hospitals. But it would be an abuse of my texts to confine the personal relationship in medicine to doctors and patients. I've said that that relationship is the very sign and symbol of the human dimension which lies at the heart of the whole profession.

It was, for instance, my privilege, early in my ministry, to get to know Professor Richard Titmuss. He was never a medical doctor, but his work will have contributed much to the Health Service. His study of blood doning called *The Gift Relationship* says much about that altruism which is at the heart of us all, but is certainly at the heart of what is best in the medical profession. One of Titmuss' most significant conclusions was that the commercialization of blood donor relationships repressed the expression of our capacity to help others. Titmuss had no doubt of the importance and priority of the personal in the Health Service.

The conviction that I have tried to express about personal relationship and the medical profession nevertheless leaves many questions unanswered today. Persons-in-relation beg the huge question, 'What is a person?' 'What *is* a human being?' Medical students have often said to me: 'I'm becoming a doctor because I can do something to serve humanity without getting bogged down in complex and insoluble problems.' But I'm afraid that won't quite do these days. Many questions are *having* to be faced, and are inescapable now, not least in research, which involve our deciding what distinguishes a human being from other animals.

I spent an afternoon recently back at Trinity College, Cambridge, with four young medical research students, all of whom are involved in genetic research at Addenbrooke's, and who simply cannot avoid fundamental questions about the very nature of our humanity – their humanity.

I note that this very day a book has been published on *Human Genetics: Choice and Responsibility*, which calls for a much wider public debate about the rights of individuals and their moral duties to people with whom they have close family or genetic ties. It says that medical ethics places enormous emphasis on the right of the patient to confidentiality, to individual choice and to the importance of respecting the patient's decision to accept or refuse treatment or screening. Clearly there are quite new and important questions to be faced in, for instance, testing genetic predisposition.

My second area of questioning concerns the Health Service itself. I am not myself sure that the management revolution in the Health Service, important and necessary as it is, is allowing personal relationships to continue to be at the very heart of the medical profession. There is good reason to wonder whether management is often becoming the master rather than the servant of the profession. Let me illustrate my anxiety with an anecdote.

Last year, I was taken into a London hospital at near to midnight. I'd suffered a minor stroke. I was taken first to A and E, and remained on a trolley there for some hours. My head protruded a little beyond the curtains, so that I was able to watch all that went on in A and E, until a bed was found for me at six the next morning. It was a Hogarthian scene that I was allowed to observe. And I was very, very grateful for those hours. I shall never doubt what doctors and nurses and other staff have to do in a central London hospital A and E on a Friday night. I can never doubt the priority of the personal there.

'Only Luke is with me' ... 'Luke, the beloved physician'.

When I was eventually wheeled into a ward, an elderly male orderly or nurse helped me to get into the bed. To my surprise, it was the very bed I had visited earlier the previous day, when it was occupied by a Gray's Inn Bencher of some distinction. The elderly orderly said to me: 'We 'ad a real gent in this bed before you.' 'Yes,' I said. 'I know.' ''Ow do you know?' he asked. 'I came to visit him,' I said. 'Why should *you* be visiting 'im?' he demanded. ''Cos it's my job,' I replied, which seemed to satisfy him – temporarily. A little while later, a female nurse came to attend to me. I *think* she was a nurse, though, as an outsider, I couldn't tell that from her dress. Uncertain, in fact, *who* she was, I asked her: 'What shall I call you?' 'Call me Joy,' she replied, breezily. 'Yes,' I said, 'I'll do that. But who is in charge of the ward?' 'No one's in charge,' she said with a smile. 'That's old-fashioned.'

I was glad of those rudimentary personal relationships at the beginning of my stay in hospital. But, after some days, I found myself asking: 'Have some of the questions we have been asking – and rightly asking – about hierarchy, and sexual prejudice, and about power and democracy, so affected not just the top surface, so to speak, of our human relating in places like hospitals, that our questioning needs now to be rather more rigorous and profound?' Someone surely needs to be clearly in charge when urgent and serious decisions have to be taken.

Put it another way. You do not need to be reminded how complex medicine is today, and how often it involves detailed, expert and sophisticated knowledge of one, perhaps minute part of a human being. How easy it can be to forget that the *end* of all our study is a human being, is *personal*. Many people may be involved in treating one person. Many of those people may never actually see the person in the ward, yet the end of all their work is a human being.

When one sort of patient carries a cash value that another sort of patient does not, so that, say, a heart transplant becomes more profitable than a hip replacement for an income-hungry hospital – income that will, nevertheless, make it possible to care for more people – I think it is right and important, without denying the intractable questions of priority that arise, to remind ourselves that human relations and human dimensions lie inalienably and irremovably at the very heart of the medical profession.

I am not suggesting we can or should ever go back to medicine as it was when, say, I was ordained. I am suggesting that in these much more complex times it is important we stand still from time to time and simply say to ourselves: the human dimension and the human relationship lie at the very heart of the medical profession and it is necessary to assert or reassert their value, and the culture which has this value at its heart. It is necessary to affirm our belief in the valuing and treating of people as ends and not as disposable means.

St Luke, who called Jesus 'Lord', nevertheless records in his Gospel stories which no one else records: the Prodigal Son, the Good Samaritan. Luke leaves us in no doubt that Jesus gave priority to the personal, and left us an example that nothing could, nothing should, supplant or replace. It is that primacy of the personal which my two texts unfailingly recall.

'Only Luke is with me' . . . 'Luke, the beloved physician'.

18

An Invitation to Heaven

Westminster Abbey; All Saints' Day, 1 November 1998

Sermons seem to arrive, as far as I'm concerned, at the most unpredictable times and often in the most inconvenient places. What I want to say to you this evening began to arrive last Tuesday when I was on Oxford station, where I had an hour to spare before being collected by a friend. I bought myself a bar of chocolate and a cup of tea, sat down at a table, and began to look at what was going on around me.

There was a group of Japanese tourists, obviously enjoying themselves hugely. They had guide books, and postcards, and were chatting away with animation. I observed a young student browsing over the week's periodicals at the bookstall. I think it was at this moment that I thought to myself, 'On Sunday evening I shall be preaching again in Westminster Abbey. I wonder how I could interest those Japanese tourists and that young man in All Saints' Day and All Souls' Day?' I munched some of my chocolate and took a few sips of the tea, and found myself turning out some of the post I'd stowed in my pockets before I left London. There was a card which invited me to my journalist friend Matthew Parris' book launch at a club called 'Heaven', near Charing Cross: a book on *Clerical Scandals*.

I picked up again the book I'd started to read in the train to Oxford, a book called *Providential Accidents*, the autobiography of Geza Vermes, an Oxford Professor who was born into a Hungarian Jewish family. He'd received a Catholic education and was later ordained priest, but his life took a different direction from what he'd expected. He married, and had a family, and ended up reasserting his Jewishness, and becoming one of the world's experts on the Dead Sea Scrolls. I thought of reading some more of the book while I waited for my friend, but the thought of this evening's sermon rather took over and I got out my notebook.

The Japanese tourists were still 'centre stage', so to speak, waiting for a London train. But it was the invitation to the book launch – which, alas, I could not go to – which shaped my first thoughts. I put down on the first page of my notebook 'An Invitation to Heaven'. It's not inconceivable that the Japanese tourists, whatever their religion, would be interested in such an invitation.

'Heaven' is in fact a gay club in London; but it's surely interesting they've called it that, with the suggestion that meeting people, getting to know them, making friends, has got something to do with our deepest needs as well as our surface ones, with our most ultimate needs and concerns and destinations: heaven.

So I sat there thinking what might be heaven for Japanese tourists – they'd clearly found something of heaven in the beauty of Oxford. And I wondered what would be heaven for that student at the bookstall, and for you and me who come to this service this particular evening. There came into my mind a poem, which is often sung here in anthem form, by the seventeenth-century poet Henry Vaughan, which has been marvellously set to music by Hubert Parry, the composer of 'Jerusalem'. And I sat there at that table at Oxford station singing it to myself:

> My soul, there is a country
>   Far beyond the stars,
> Where stands a wingèd sentry
>   All skilful in the wars.
> There, above noise and danger –
>   Sweet Peace sits crowned with smiles,
> And One born in a manger
>   Commands the beauteous files.
> He is thy gracious friend
>   And – O my soul, awake! –
> Did in pure love descend
>   To die here for thy sake.
> If thou canst get but thither,
>   There grows the flower of Peace,
> The Rose that cannot wither,
>   Thy fortress, and thy ease.

> Leave then thy foolish ranges,
>   For none can thee secure
> But one who never changes,
>   Thy God, thy Life, thy Cure.

I may have sung a little out loud, for the woman at the next table looked at me as though I was slightly mad. I gave her a smile and just restrained myself from saying: 'Don't worry, dear, I've been responding to an invitation to heaven. Would you like one?' But I realized it was time to get up and see whether my kind friend had arrived. He did arrive within minutes, and I was carried off to talk for an hour about Bishop Trevor Huddleston, who died on the Sunday after Easter this year. Bishop Trevor I knew well as a friend. He wasn't a saint, but I was very glad to be talking about him on the way towards All Saints'-tide this year. He's had his invitation to heaven, which he answered by living a life concerned for justice, not least in South Africa. I couldn't possibly leave him out of my thoughts on All Saints' Day and All Souls' Eve this year.

I didn't get a chance to think further about what to say this evening for a couple of days, and when I read over what I'd written, it occurred to me that there's one word for that phrase 'invitation to heaven' and that's 'vocation', and another which is identical – 'calling'. St Paul addresses the Christians at Rome as those who are literally 'called to be *saints*'. Called to be saints – an invitation to heaven.

Trevor Huddleston, when he was Bishop of Masasi, in Tanzania, in the 1960s, came back from that poverty-stricken African diocese to conduct a Mission to Oxford University. No one who was present at his addresses has ever forgotten them. He ended his last address with these words:

> *Vocation!* Is there really any way of saying to an audience what it means to each one within that audience?
>
> Vocation! It is – somehow – like 'service' or 'commitment', a rather dangerous word. It is so easy to talk, and even to think, of '*my* vocation' – as though it was something upon which I confer a dignity and glory by accepting it.
>
> But what is it really? Remember the Early Churches – Laodicea is one of them, the least attractive – not unlike some of our Christian churches today. 'I know thy works, that thou art neither cold nor hot ... so because thou art lukewarm, and neither hot nor cold, I will spew thee out of my mouth.' Not a very encouraging thing to hear. And it

gets even worse. 'Thou sayest I am rich (and have gotten riches) and have need of nothing; and knowest not that thou art wretched and miserable and poor and blind and naked.'

Yet it is to *this* church: to this group of Christians – lukewarm in their faith, wretched, miserable, poor, blind and naked in their life as Christians – that the most winning words in the whole of Scripture are addressed:

'Behold, I stand at the door and knock: if any man hear my voice and open the door, I will come in to him and will sup with him, and he with me.'

Vocation! What is it – really? *My* life? *My* activity? *My* decision? *My* way?

It is none of these. It is Jesus, the Lord, the True and Living God, standing, knocking, waiting. That is all.

So this All Saints' Day I don't really want to talk about, say, Trevor Huddleston's vocation or mine! I want to remind you and to remind myself that every one of us has a *vocation*, is *called* by the Living God to be a saint.

Does this include the Japanese tourists that were in my mind when I began my thoughts for this evening, and the student at the bookstall? Yes, it does. Though their invitations to heaven may be coming to them a different way from mine.

Only a few weeks ago I went back to Trinity College in Cambridge where I was chaplain in the 1950s, and when I went into the chapel, I found there were 46 brass plates on the wall to commemorate Fellows of the College whom I had known there as friends, but who had since died, including, for instance, Bishop John Robinson, who wrote the bestseller *Honest to God* in the 1960s and whom I'd known as a close friend. But most of the Fellows were not what I will call 'paid up Christians'. They were historians, such as G. M. Trevelyan, and atomic physicists, such as Otto Frisch, and musicians such as Ralph Vaughan Williams, and Martin Ryle who designed radio telescopes for astronomy. In a way they were, most of them, secular saints. I can't possibly forget them at All Saints' and All Souls'-tide. You can't forget friends.

Sir Walter Raleigh said: 'Everyone comes to God by his secret stair.' I treasure that saying. And it makes me want to add another word to the list of words that cluster around 'invitation to heaven' and 'calling' and 'vocation'. I want to add the word 'journey'. I wonder whether I would have prepared the sermon I have prepared for you this evening if I hadn't been on a station, surrounded by people who were travelling, going on journeys. All Saints, All Souls, are on a journey. We all are. It wasn't just John Bunyan who was on a Pilgrim's Progress. The Japanese tourists were, and the lad at the bookstall. And the man from Hungary whose autobiography I'm reading, Geza Vermes, who significantly called his autobiography *Providential Accidents* – things which had happened to him on his journey.

One of the saints of our time who would, I'm sure, speak to those Japanese tourists was Dag Hammarskjøld, the Swedish Secretary-General of the United Nations from 1953 to 1961, when his plane crashed in the heart of Africa. Hammarskjøld had a critical attitude to religion in his early years, not least to the Christian religion. But he became a man who was not only familiar with the Christian mystics but was clearly a mystic himself. In his spiritual journal, that's to say, the diary of his spiritual journey, published after his death with the title *Markings*, he wrote words which make it quite clear how important the idea of life as a journey was to him. His very first entry in *Markings* has this paragraph:

> I am being driven forward
> Into an unknown land.
> The pass grows steeper,
> The air colder and sharper,
> A wind from my unknown goal
> Stirs the strings
> Of expectation.
> Still the question:
> Shall I ever get there?
> There where life resounds,
> A clear pure note
> In the silence.

This was Hammarskjøld's response to an 'invitation to heaven'.

In his journal for Whitsunday 1961, Hammerskjøld wrote of what had happened, not long before he took on the job of Secretary-General to the United Nations:

> I don't know who or what put the question. I don't know when it was put. I don't even remember answering. But at some moment I did answer Yes to Someone – or Something – and from that hour I was certain that existence is meaningful and that, therefore, my life, in self-

surrender, had a goal ... As I continued along the Way, I learned, step by step, word by word, that behind every sentence spoken by the hero of the Gospels, stands one man and one man's experience.

Two months before his plane crashed in Central Africa, he wrote:

> Give us
> A pure heart
> That we may see Thee
> A humble heart
> That we may hear Thee;
> A heart of Love
> That we may serve Thee,
> A heart of faith
> That we may live Thee
> Thou
> Whom I do not know
> But whose I am
> Thou
> Whom I do not comprehend
> But Who has dedicated me
> To my fate
> Thou

Dag Hammarskjøld travelled hundreds of thousands of miles in the cause of world peace, to Japan, China, Suez, Thailand, the Congo. He never found a home in any one church, but he wrote from his own experience.

> The longest journey
> Is the journey inwards

All Saints have known that. All Souls need to discover it.

Japanese tourists on a station and a student browsing periodicals. You and I. We've all received our invitation to heaven, we are all called to be saints and are all on our journey; on which, no doubt, there have been 'providential accidents'.

19

Remembrance Day 1998

Westminster Abbey; 8 November 1998

November is the month of memory, beginning with All Saints' Day on 1 November and All Souls' Day the next day, and now Remembrance Day. Someone said to me a few days ago: 'How do you find something fresh to say every Remembrance Day?' Well, I have to say, I've never found it a problem, because every year something happens to remind me afresh of the meaning of Remembrance Day. And this year has been no exception.

In July, I conducted the memorial service of Major Michael Hammond-Maude of the Iniskilling Dragoon Guards. And this evening I'd like to tell you something of his story, because I believe it has something to say to us all, not only about him but about all those, known and unknown, whom we remember today in this Abbey that holds the shrine of the Unknown Warrior.

I last saw Michael earlier this year, just before he died, in a nursing home in Pimlico. He had something like Alzheimer's Disease, that afflicts the aged, and he hardly recognized me in his last weeks.

I didn't myself know Michael until 1981, when my friend since 1955, John Robinson, later Bishop of Woolwich, went to live at Arncliffe, in Yorkshire, where Michael was living. Somewhat surprisingly, for they were two very different characters, a friendship sprang up between the Bishop and Michael, who might have been the squire of Arncliffe in other days. It was a friendship which lasted until Bishop John's death in 1983. What I have to say this evening arises from my friendship with Michael. It will also stem from Michael's private papers and from the generosity of his wife, Sonia, who let me see those papers.

I want to read you now quite an extensive extract from Michael's diary which he kept, particularly for his mother, in 1940. Michael wrote:

In the morning of the 18 May 1940, the Belgian Army, part of the French Army, and the English, are retreating back towards the west. My regiment is part of the rearguard, and the squadron in which I am lieutenant has received the order to take up a defensive line on the west, just outside the city of Brussels. Three light reconnaissance tanks and another similar one have been left under my command, at Berchem St Agathe, to observe and to prevent, as far as possible, the advance of the German troops . . .

The railway station at Berchem is 800 metres behind us in a small valley. It is 9.30 a.m. and all is calm. My tank is on the crossroad which goes down to the level crossing at the station. I have just received the map position of the main body of the squadron where we must go when we withdraw. Around 9.45 I see a civilian approaching my tank who appears to be extremely on edge. He informs me that there are some Germans who have just arrived in the station behind us. At 10.00 I decide to send three tanks to the station, to report on the situation. Five minutes later they return, and the lieutenant of the section tells me there are around six anti-tank guns, well camouflaged and in position at the station, which is on the right hand side as you go down the main road. He adds that the barrier on the level crossing is down. There is only one thing to do, and that is to withdraw to the other side of the valley and to shoot at the gunners with our machine guns . . . The tanks are completely closed tight, but I can hear the noise of their machine guns as they approach the station. All is going well! The first tank has had to cross the level crossing . . . We are moving at about 65km per hour and we are not more than 200 metres from the level crossing . . .

All of a sudden there is an astounding noise and I can feel a huge knock against my left leg. At the same time I hear a cry of pain from my gunner, sat to my left. The turret is surrounded by black smoke, the damaged engine no longer works, and the tank comes to a stop. Thoughtlessly, I open the small hatch above my head and manage to climb out of the tank. Perched on the open hatch, I realize that my left leg is immobile, and I fall two metres, on to the ground. We are in a garden, ten metres from a small red house. I hear the voice of my driver, who asks how I am. He says that he himself is OK. We crawl up to the steps of the house, and there I fall into semi-consciousness, and can only remember half of the following events.

The motor-cyclist of my section, who stayed next to the tank, and who is not at all injured, comes to see us . . . I learn from him that the gunner is so badly injured that it is impossible to get him out of the tank. A very short moment after, I hear a gun shot, and the motor-cyclist falls dead beside me. I can only suppose that he killed himself rather than be taken prisoner ... Soon, several Germans arrive with an officer. They treat us very correctly. Very carefully, they pull the gunner from the tank and place him on the ground, covered by a jacket .... . I remember that the Germans gave us cigarettes, and I was astonished that those of the officer were a very expensive English brand which can only be found rarely in England.

In the meantime, several Belgian civilians arrived, and I especially remember two of them: a young lady who was tending to my comrades, and a young girl who had my head resting on her knees for six hours, until the ambulance took us to Brussels. She left, after thanking us for what we had done for her country.

During the afternoon, a German doctor arrived, bandaged my leg, and gave each of us an anti-tetanus injection. Until then, I had felt nothing in my leg, but at that moment I started to feel a dull pain. During the afternoon, I learned that the gunner was dead, but I didn't come to terms with the fact until several days later ... At 5.00, an ambulance arrived and four of us were put inside – the driver, two injured Belgians, and myself. It appeared to me that we drove for around two hours. Finally, we stopped outside the Palais Royal which during the war was being used as an auxiliary hospital. The nurses on the door told the German officer who was in the ambulance that the doctors would not be able to operate immediately, and that they would have to take us elsewhere. By an amazing stroke of luck, there was at that time an ambulance from the Red Cross clinic which had brought some medications to the Palais Royal. The nurse who was with the ambulance, on seeing my leg, which was sticking out of the rear door, told the Germans to follow her to the clinic. Half an hour later, we arrived. I vaguely remember the voices of the nurses who were cutting my clothes, and who seemed to be in a hurry ... I really was under the impression that I was going to die. I can honestly say that I couldn't have cared less, as I was so tired ...

I cannot remember a great deal of the eight days following. I must have been operated on twice: once for the amputation, and a second time to remove the shrapnel from my thigh ... On the eighth day Dr George Brolée put on the first bandage, an operation which I will never forget. It was only whilst I was in the bandaging room that I realized that they had managed to save my knee, although there was talk of amputating it at the thigh, because of so many deep wounds which I had. From that moment onwards, I was on the road to a complete recovery, and, thanks to the magnificent care of the doctors and nurses, this took no time at all.

I realize that was a very long extract, but I suspect you will feel as privileged to have heard those words as I to read them. They tell us so much. Of course, they don't yet make a sermon, but they do say some important things to us all about our God-given humanity. And I think it's worth just noting them, and asking a few reflective questions about them.

Where does human courage come from? and endurance? The German soldiers were kind to Michael. Where does our human capacity for kindness come from?

The Belgian nurses and the German doctor looked after Michael, and the Red Cross ambulance people. Our capacity to care for one another is a wonderful revelation of God-in-us. The work of the Red Cross is a working out of Jesus' story of the Good Samaritan.

In fact, I've only told you a fragment of Michael's story. And I must tell you that at that time, while Michael was under fire, his mother was living in what was sometimes called 'bomb alley', not far from Tunbridge Wells, in Kent.

In May 1940, the first she knew of what had happened to Michael was that one of her letters to him was returned to her marked 'deceased'. And, on a day when several bombs had fallen nearby, she received the telegram 'Missing believed killed in action on 18 May'. Then, on 23 May, she received a letter of confirmation from the War Office, and on 2 June, another wire from the War Office correcting their first wire to 'Killed in action', with yet another letter of confirmation two days later. Michael's mother therefore put an obituary in *The Times* on 13 June 1940. A letter of condolence was received from the king and other letters poured in which she answered. But then, on 19 June, she got a rather apologetic letter from the War Office saying that, from further information, they now went back to 'Missing believed killed in action'. But not until August – 5 August – did Michael's mother receive another letter from the War Office. I will read what she wrote in her diary:

> I thought it was just to say that now you were to be considered 'Killed in action'. I opened it quite casually, and then – my darling boy – it said: news has come from the British Military Attaché in Berne that an American ambulance worker had reported you were in Brussels, wounded, but recovering well. I could hardly believe it, and did not tell anyone for a day, I was so afraid it mightn't be true, and that I musn't say it out loud! You will never know what that news meant to us both …

Michael did not waste time when he was a prisoner of war. He spent some time perfecting his French and German, so that eventually he became the camp interpreter. As an amputee, he couldn't, of course, escape, but he did help those who escaped by organizing escape routes, digging tunnels, and so on. At one time he was supposed to be involved in an exchange of prisoners. He was put on a train to go home, and was taken all the way to the port, only to be returned again to camp.

There's no doubting Michael's courage. When eventually he was repatriated in 1944, he was asked by a British officer in the camp to take back an important message to the British goverment. This he did – in the hollow socket of his artificial leg. On top of the message was placed a layer of ordinary dust. Although he was asked to remove his artificial leg, the message was never discovered. Heaven knows what would have happened to Michael had it been found.

When I think of Michael's mother, I think of her courage, and of that other God-given quality we call hope.

But, of course, there are other things that story forces us to reflect upon. No one can doubt that it was great wickedness which caused that war, and goes on causing wars in the world, with people shooting at each other and bombing one another. Our human capacity for evil is huge, but it's so curiously mixed with our capacity for good, and our capacity to be horrified by atrocities.

Recently, the new German Prime Minister has been visiting Britain, so there's another capacity to reflect on: the God-given capacity for reconciliation, made manifest most clearly in Jesus himself – the capacity for right to triumph over wrong, good over evil, truth over the lie.

But Michael's story has one other message for us. Had that shell been a fraction of an inch closer to Michael, I would never have known him. The whole of his life, his marriage, his children – the whole of his life from 1940 to 1998 – depended on a fraction of an inch.

It was the circumstances of war that made Michael's life so precarious. But it would be foolish to think that our lives are not precarious. Maybe they're not *so* precarious. But throughout all our life, from fertilization of the cells that enable us to be born, to birth itself, and then a thousand, indeed a million other ingredients of our existence, make it precarious. But we take our security for granted instead of, from time to time, reflecting on our God-given precariousness. And Michael's precarious life that was saved in 1940 was saved for only 58 years more. Death came to him this year, as it will come to us all.

These days of November – All Saints' Day, All Souls' Day and Remembrance Day – have an important message for us all. They provide an invitation to us all to commit ourselves again into the hands of our loving Creator, who will never cease his love and care for us either in this world or the next.

20

The Amnesty Service

Salisbury Cathedral; 12 December 1998

When I received the kind invitation from the Dean to preach today, he made it clear that this service, and each event of the extended weekend, is an entity; yet those who planned the weekend saw it also as a unity: beginning with Francis Grier's *Mass in Time of Persecution* on Thursday evening – as, in part, a preparation for this annual Amnesty Service; and the service this year having also in mind the fiftieth anniversary of the Declaration of Human Rights. Then, this evening, the performance of Michael Tippett's *A Child of Our Time*. And, before it, the Sunday Eucharist.

Was there one text, I wondered, that might articulate this unity – and, indeed, be a bond of unity to the separate and several events? What, after reflection, suggested itself surprised me by its simplicity and yet its profundity. It was a verse from today's reading from the book of Genesis: 'On the day when God created human beings he made them in his own likeness.'

The persecuted – the subject of Francis Grier's Mass – God created 'in his own likeness'. So, too, were all those on Amnesty International's appallingly long lists. All human rights concern the rights of those God created 'in his own likeness'. And any child of our time, every child of our time, has been made in God's own likeness. As I said, I was surprised by the simplicity yet the profundity of that text. But, of course, it's not as simple as it seems: because we who are made in the likeness of God can and do perpetrate the most horrific acts of inhumanity. Made in God's own likeness, we are yet capable of untold barbarity.

If the mystery of our creation is the primal mystery, close to it must be not some piece of Augustinian theology of the Fall, but the tale of our experience – and our fellow human beings' experience – of the mystery of evil. Yet the experience of evil is not the last word. The first creative word, of God's image and likeness in human beings, in humanity, is always being uttered, and is never defeated. Its ultimate defeat would be the death of God. But, for the most part, we who gather in this cathedral today know that God is not dead; for we know ourselves to be made in God's image and likeness, and that we live in him, or, at least, partly live in him, so that in every phase of history – personal, national, international – that is evidently the truth. And of this truth, I want to suggest, the life of Michael Tippett is itself a wonderfully illuminating illustration, though his personal pilgrimage of faith ended in agnosticism.

It is well known that his homosexuality made Tippett aware of being an outsider, even an outcast. Yet, to quote his own words, he became 'quite certain that ... somewhere music could have a direct relation also to the compassion that was so deep in my heart'. When, in the 1930s, Tippett saw, for the first time, the undernourished children of the north of England, he said he was 'ashamed'. And, visiting a children's home in Bavaria, set up to help those abandoned on the streets of Berlin, when the Allies of the First World War continued their blockade, the seeds of *A Child of Our Time*, and of his opera *A New Year*, were sown. But, truth to tell, those seeds were sown when he was made in the likeness of God. They were his human and divine inheritance. And it's not just curious, it's profoundly significant that it was on 3 September 1939 – the very day the Second World War began – that Tippett started to write *A Child of Our Time*.

Though he walked wounded, vulnerable and guilt-ridden, Tippett knew he had to express his solidarity with the oppressed and the despised. It was, in fact, 'Crystal Night', 9 November 1938, which had first aroused in Tippett the horror from which *A Child of Our Time* began. Our horror of inhumanity – our own and that of others – is one of God's best gifts to us and in us; one of the best witnesses to our origin; one of the best weapons in defence of human rights.

A Child of Our Time was modelled on Handel's *Messiah* and on the Bach Passions, not least because it is in the roughness of human history – and not least in the history of 'Our Time' – that the despised and rejected, and the scapegoats of society, are to be found. Yet it is from among them that redemption and the Redeemer raises his head: from the image and likeness of God-in-humanity. So Tippett selected his images from a wide diversity of sources: Blake,

Wilfred Owen, Carl Gustav Jung, T. S. Eliot – all that would articulate the mystery and glory of humanity; the mystery of *in*humanity and of compassion; of darkness and of light. In 'Behold the Man', from *A Child of Our Time*, he echoed, of set purpose, Isaiah's and Handel's 'Behold the lamb'. 'I would know my shadow and my light, so shall I at last be whole' is the Jungian prayer that emanates from Tippet's own profound experience as an individual and as a member of humanity.

Tippett's mother, let us record, was a suffragette, for which cause she went to prison; and you feel that her witness and sense of social obligation taught her son, and thus some of us, about polemic and protest allied to the great truths of our human nature and being, and thus to human rights.

You will, I hope, forgive me, if I admit to a kind of local pride in Tippett, because I live but a stone's throw from Morley College, in Lambeth, where Tippett was Director of Music for many years. And in 1940, when the College was hit by a land mine, I was myself working not far away, at a riverside wharf on the south bank of the Thames; and, even in those dark days, when musical life in London was near to its lowest ebb, Tippett, in 1942–3, experimented with concerts, with choir and orchestra, that were themselves a living act of faith-in-resurrection. He saw it as his vocation at such a time – in God-like mood – to create music, as a way of saving the world from destruction. It was his 'peace work', so to speak, in the midst of war. It was his witness to his origins.

There is a kind of parable even in the fact that after Morley College was hit, it was Tippett who found, amid the rubble, some library copies of the Purcell Society Edition; and, studying those at leisure, he was stimulated by the characteristics of that music, such as the ground bass with variations. It was another aspect – another allegory – of resurrection.

The title *A Child of Our Time* was, of course, chosen by Tippett only after much thought. Tippett was often concerned with the mystery of time – indeed, he placarded that mystery before us as another of the great mysteries of existence itself. Time itself Tippett sets forth as literally a working, a mysterious, creation of God. It's not altogether surprising that a composer whose raw material is not only sound – and silence – but time should teach us to use the material of time as the vehicle of the divine.

Tippett was, of course, 'a child of our time'. He composed also what he carefully called *The Mask of Time*, which focuses on man's instinct to survive, as part of the human God-given mystery.

But the mystery of time for Tippett includes also the mystery of mortality:

> O man: make peace with your mortality
> For this too is God

one of the actors in *The Mask of Time* proclaims. *A Child of Our Time* ends with the Spiritual 'Deep River': 'Deep River, my home is over Jordan'. Each one of us has to cross that deep river sometime. That is the mystery of mortality.

But it was not only in his composing that Tippett confronted the mystery of time. When he went to prison for his pacifist principles he was living out time – 'doing time' – as he believed it had to be lived out. (Needless to say, he studied Bach's *Art of Fugue* in prison, and tried to help with the small prison orchestra – besides, of course, sewing mailbags!)

I am trying to say, as we meet together today with our concern for human rights and for those with whom Amnesty International is concerned, that there is hardly anyone who can better show us how to be a child of our time, and how to be concerned for human rights, than Tippett. But in order to be that, we have ourselves to confront the human mysteries, and not least the mystery of time, in order to be human. And I suggest that the approach of the millennium, whatever else it does, calls each one of us to confront and attempt to plumb the mystery of time – that profoundly human mystery.

Not only the composers but the poets will help us. Tippett's friendship with T. S. Eliot was the biggest influence in his entire career. He described Eliot as his 'spiritual father'. Originally, he asked Eliot to write the libretto for *A Child of Our Time*, but eventually Eliot advised him it would be better for him to produce his own text.

In Shakespeare's writings there are nearly 200 separate sentences each of which expresses a different thought on time. Whatever his religion, Shakespeare makes it clear that to be human you have to confront the mystery of time.

It is, of course, in time that the mystery of good and the mystery of evil are revealed.

A few nights ago, I was invited to a meal with a West London vicar whom I hardly knew. He invited another guest, a woman whom I'd never met. Her name was Annabel Markov. I learned gradually that she was the widow of Georgi Markov, the Bulgarian novelist who had been imprisoned as a student for his beliefs but, in 1971, came to England, and joined the World Service of the BBC as Bulgarian Correspondent. On 7 September 1978, some of you will remember, he was shot by an assassin, on Waterloo Bridge, with a minuscule pellet of a rare and deadly poison, by means of what looked like an umbrella. Markov was shot for telling the terrible truth about his country - a child of our time. The book of his memoirs, published in 1983, and called *The Truth that Kills*, is one I shall now never forget. How many children of our time have been martyrs to the truth that kills!

The mystery of man created in the likeness of God but who nevertheless is capable, and more than capable, of unspeakable inhumanity: is that the whole story? No, surely not. The whole story includes the resistance, like that of Georgi Markov – and the redemption.

Whenever now I come to this beautiful cathedral – which itself, as a building, says something about human beings being made in God's own likeness – I always make my way to the East End: to the Prisoners of Conscience window that is now the East Window, in the Trinity Chapel, as we shall all do soon together. A former Dean of the cathedral, Sydney Evans, who was my chaplain when I was a student, nearly 50 years ago, and became my lifelong friend, had a vision. 'In this twentieth century,' he wrote, 'there have always been individuals and small groups who have kept alight candles of freedom: men and women who have challenged the easy assumption that might confers right, who have stood firm for truth against the lie. These individuals, now so numerous, a few known by name, countless others whose names are unknown, have come to be spoken of as "Prisoners of Conscience". Who else in this twentieth century of frightfulness could be more appropriately commemorated in a new window in an ancient cathedral than the men and women who, at the cost of mental anguish, physical pain, spiritual humiliation, isolation or premature death, have upheld by non-violent witness the dignity of the human person against falsehood and tyranny?'

Sydney Evans, in his description of Gabriel Loire's window, says: 'The two outside lancets remember and symbolize those who stand for truth against the lie in circumstances of political pressure. The central group of three lancets presents Jesus of Nazareth as himself a prisoner of conscience, suffering the consequences of his stand in humiliation, physical pain and crucifixion, but vindicated in the experience which the Christian Community of Faith affirms to be the supreme disclosure of the way things really are, a revealing of the mystery of ultimate reality.' He goes on: 'The gold symbolizes the glory of God radiant to eyes of faith even in degradation ... The gold in the glass declares God's vindication and validation of all that Jesus said and did and endured, and also vindicates and validates all that is of truth and love in the stand of all prisoners of conscience ... Evil turned into goodness by love, falsehood overcome by suffering-allegiance-to-truth; these are the fundamental affirmations of the window ...' 'Each of us,' he says, 'in our individual way, will know ourselves being searched in the deep centre of our being ...'

When God made us in his likeness; when he made good and evil; when he gave us time, he also set before us the mystery of the redeeming of time. It is grappling with that mystery of redemption which is also involved in confronting the mystery of our humanity.

Whenever I hear, as I shall hear this evening, the great Spiritual, for Chorus and Bass Solo, in *A Child of Our Time* – 'Go down, Moses' – I always now hear it as a call to commit myself again, alongside Christ the Redeemer, and alongside all those whom Dietrich Bonhoeffer called 'the suffering God in the life of the world', because when we are created in the likeness of God by his creative power, we are created also to share in his work of redemption. Needing to be redeemed, we dare to believe that in our full God-given humanity we are part of his redemptive life.

> Go down, Moses, way down in Egypt's land:
> Tell old Pharaoh to let my people go.

That is the fundamental call to restore human rights, to restore human dignity, to restore humanity itself.

'On the day when God created human beings he made them in his own likeness.' And he is still creating human beings in his own likeness, and yet more wonderfully restoring them to that likeness, and using us as his partners in that work; for to be 'in his likeness' is to be in the likeness of the Redeemer.

'On the day when God created human beings he made them in his own likeness.'

21

Power and Influence

University College, Oxford
21 February 1999

'He returned in the power of the Spirit into Galilee.'
Luke 4.14

It's difficult for me to believe that it's over 25 years since I last preached here. I remember the occasion as though it were yesterday. I came to preach on the evening of Ash Wednesday. At dinner, I sat next to the then Master, Lord Redcliffe-Maud. My eyes wandered down the table to the portrait of Lord Beveridge. It so happened I'd been reading Beveridge's autobiography, which he'd called *Power and Influence*. I'd been highly impressed by its very first page, in the course of which he said that, since he came to manhood, he'd seldom been without influence but as seldom had he power.

Those two words – power and influence – were clearly very important to Beveridge. Power to him meant government: making laws and enforcing them, but it included the control of money. Influence meant persuasion: appealing to reason. Beveridge quoted George Washington's dictum: 'Influence is not government.' For a man who was responsible for the Beveridge Report – which so radically altered our Welfare State – and who was for eighteen years Director of the London School of Economics, and was for seven years Master of this College, I thought it curious, to say the least, for Beveridge to say he had never had power.

I shared my thoughts with Lord Redcliffe-Maud. He smiled, and said: 'Of course, Beveridge always wanted power. He only had influence.' That didn't really deal with my point: that Beveridge had power. But at the end of the meal, as we walked over to the chapel,

Lord Redcliffe-Maud said: 'I feel I've been rather uncharitable to you about my predecessor, Beveridge. By way of amends, I'll have a certain document put in your room.'

Later, when the service in chapel was over, I retired to bed, to find in my room a copy of the Inaugural Lecture to the Royal Statistical Society by Harold Wilson, recently, of course, Prime Minister, and a former Research Fellow of this college. I was somewhat daunted by the fact that I had to read a lecture to the Royal Statistical Society, even though it *was* the beginning of the penitential season. But I needn't have worried. The lecture was entirely given over to a most moving personal tribute to Beveridge by Harold Wilson who, when he was a Research Fellow here, had been in the care of Beveridge. There was no doubt whatever of the *influence* Beveridge had had on the future Prime Minister. I could not possibly say it was 'only' influence he had had. But I remember wondering whether perhaps we should carefully distinguish – without dividing - those two words 'power' and 'influence'.

I've now reached my 'anecdotage' in life: so I fear that was a rather long introduction to what I want to say this evening, by way of comment on my text, which, describing the return of Jesus after his Lent – his forty days and forty nights in the wilderness – says: 'He returned in the power of the Spirit into Galilee.' It was, of course, that word 'power' – the power of the Spirit – which caught my attention. What kind of power was 'the power of the Spirit'? Was it power or influence? There's a hymn by Harriet Auber which says of the Holy Spirit:

> He came sweet influence to impart,
> A gracious willing guest,
> While he can find one humble heart
> Wherein to rest.

Does the Holy Spirit 'only have influence'?

In the New Testament there are, in fact, several words which describe the power of God at work in the world. And the second movement of my sermon, so to speak, must be a kind of Adagio (or should I say Lent-o?) in which I reflect out loud on one or two of those words.

The Greek word which is used for power in the verse that forms my text, 'He returned in the power of the Spirit', is *dunamis*, from which we get the word *dynamic*. 'He returned in the dynamism – the dynamic power – of the Holy Spirit' wouldn't be a bad translation.

But there's another Greek word for power which is used often in the New Testament: *exousia*, derived or conferred or transmitted power; in other words, authority. When Jesus is recorded as saying 'All authority in heaven and on earth is given unto me', the Greek word used is *exousia*, though the English versions most often simply say 'power'. It's not difficult to illustrate those two very different meanings of the same word 'power'.

> A butcher may have the power to kill a couple of pigs; with his strength he could kill ten and still feel able to kill more. But at the moment the government won't give him the power to kill one.

There's often a conflict between dynamic power and legal power. But the problem of power is rarely as simple as that. St Paul says: 'The powers that be are ordained by God', but he also says, 'We wrestle not against flesh and blood.' In his theology the world outside this world was alive with powers – angelic powers, and so on – but Jesus was now above all those powers. He'd got them beaten. I wonder what you think are the powers that influence you?

Music? Experts in your subject? Examination authorities? Parents? Politicians? The media? Jesus? What others think? Sex? Your bank manager? Truth? Friends?

In any society of standing power is, of course, complex. Dominant personalities who innovate and renovate, the natural leaders, have an authority of their own. People who hold certain hereditary offices, or certain elected offices, have an authority of their own. The purpose which motivates the society has an authority of its own, whether that purpose be the building of a classless society or a democracy. Standard norms of conduct are another form of authority. Shared traditions form part of the authoritative guidance to society. Customs have a similar part in the control and direction of society. All these, and many other elements, play their part in the complex web of authority; and, because the limits of each authority are rarely laid down precisely, there are almost inevitably conflicts of authority. 'Ye have heard it said of old time ... but I say unto you.' When traditions or myths are outworn by repetition to the point of weariness, and the innovator comes along with 'new myths for old', there may be conflict. The conflict of authority – of authorities, of powers and influences – is always with us. To live is to evaluate and choose our authorities, our powers, our influences. That's what human freedom is.

Well, the Adagio is over. Before the last movement let me repeat the theme that I sounded at the beginning: 'He returned in the power of the Spirit into Galilee.' How is the power of God – the power of the Spirit of God – made manifest? Another hymn, this time by John Keble, speaking of the Spirit, says:

> It fills the Church of God; it fills
> The sinful world around:
> Only in stubborn hearts and wills
> No place for it is found.

Frank Field, very much a committed Christian in politics, in his Beveridge Memorial Lecture last year as Minister of State for Welfare Reform – before he vacated that office and its power – said: 'Beveridge was part of that band of public servants who deployed their talents, not for personal financial gain, but to the advancement of the public good.' Beveridge died in 1963.

Harold Wilson, in his Beveridge Memorial Lecture, described Beveridge as 'the greatest administrative genius of this century, and one of the greatest social reformers in our entire history.' Harold Wilson died in 1995.

Lord Redcliffe-Maud – another dedicated Christian – died in 1982 after a lifetime of public service, not least reforming local government, but also as a memorable High Commissioner to South Africa.

To some it may seem strange that I should now set those men of your college alongside Jesus, who 'returned in the power of the Spirit into Galilee'. But I do that of set purpose because, surely, we should set ourselves alongside Jesus, comparing and contrasting ourselves with him: with Jesus, with whom we are flesh and blood, who set aside forty days and forty nights at the beginning of his adult life, to resolve what kind of life he should lead. And then there was teaching, story telling and work done in the name and the power of God, until after probably only three years, he went up to Jerusalem – to the Temple and the Last Supper, to Gethsemane and the Crucifixion.

Jesus lived a brief life of power in subordination to love, but that life led to suffering and death. All his life was lived in the power of the Spirit of God, not only in Galilee but in Gethsemane and Golgotha. So that when the Fourth Gospel came to be written, the author recorded Jesus saying of his life, just before he died: 'It is finished, achieved, accomplished.'

That's, of course, what the Christian believes God would want us to be able to say through the power of the Spirit of God in us: which drove Jesus from the wilderness into Galilee.

22

Psalm 130

St Martin-in-the-Fields; 31 March 1999

I feel privileged to be invited to preach in this series on 'Reading the Bible with Imagination'. I've chosen to base what I say on a psalm – Psalm 130, and I've chosen a psalm for several reasons. The first is because the psalms were very clearly Jesus' own prayer book or, at least, a very important part of it, and I've always had the feeling that 'if the psalms were good enough for Jesus, they should be good enough for me'.

In 1946, when I was 21, I came across a book called *The Psalms in Human Life* by Rowland Prothero, a writer and an MP. It was published 90 years ago, and describes how different people in different circumstances have found the psalms valuable, and tells you that about each psalm. No one, after reading it, could ever doubt that the psalms have been very valuable to very different people at very different times.

Psalm 130 is my choice of psalm today, Passion Sunday. The Prayer Book version begins: 'Out of the deep have I called unto thee, O Lord'. It's known – by the Latin of its opening words – as the *De Profundis:* 'De profundis clamo ad te ...' Which makes me say, in passing, that I find it useful to use different versions and translations of the psalms. I like to get near the original meaning of the text; but that may not be the most beautiful or the most memorable. 'De profundis clamo ad te' sounds beautiful to me. And human beings are people whose imagination responds to beauty as well as to truth, so I think it's important to ring the changes on the versions of the psalms we use.

The *De Profundis* is still used by Roman Catholics in their Office for the Departed, rather as the Burial Sentences are used in the

Anglican Prayer Book. So it's not surprising that Cardinal Newman, in *The Dream of Gerontius* – so marvellously set to music by Elgar – puts the words 'Sanctus fortis, sanctus deus, *de profundis* oro te' into the mouth of the dying Gerontius. And Martin Luther gave the German people one of their most memorable hymns, based on this psalm, upon which Bach built one of his finest chorales: 'Aus tiefer Noth schrei ich zu dir'. It was this psalm which John Wesley heard sung as an anthem in St Paul's Cathedral on the afternoon of Wednesday 24 May 1738, that attuned his heart to receive the assurance of salvation that evening in a room in Aldersgate Street. And Oscar Wilde, in the loneliness of his imprisonment in Reading Gaol, wrote to his friend Bosey that letter which is one long cry of pain, and simply put at its head the two words *De Profundis*.

Let me refer to one other person to whom this particular psalm has meant much; the theologian Paul Tillich, an outspoken critic of Nazism, who left Germany to teach and preach in the United States. In his book of sermons *The Shaking of the Foundations*, he has a sermon on 'The Depths of Existence', and at the head of it there is the first verse of this psalm. In that great sermon Tillich first of all looks at how we use the words 'deep' and 'depth' in daily life – in poetry, philosophy, and in the Bible – to indicate a spiritual attitude, though the words are taken from a spatial experience. 'Deep,' he says, 'in its spiritual use has two meanings: it means either the opposite of shallow or the opposite of high. Truth is deep and not shallow; suffering is depth and not height. The light of truth and the darkness of suffering are deep. There is a depth in God, and there is a depth out of which the psalmist cries to God. 'Why is truth deep? Why is suffering deep?' Tillich asks. 'Surface,' he says , 'is that side of things which first appears to us ... Yet if we act according to what things and persons *seem* to be, we are disappointed ... so we try to penetrate below the surface in order to learn what things really are. Why have men always asked for truth?' What an extraordinary human characteristic it is – Tillich observes – 'the pursuit of truth. What a remarkable human gift and attribute.'

Tillich has a passage on what we nowadays call 'depth psychology'. And then he writes what I think is one of the very great theological and spiritual passages of our times. He says: 'The name of this infinite and inexhaustible depth and ground of all being is *God*. That depth is what the word *God* means. And if that word has not much meaning for you, translate it, and speak of the depths of your life, of the source of your being, of your ultimate concern, of what you take seriously without any reservation ... if you know that God means depth, you know much about Him ... He who knows about depth knows about God.' Tillich then goes on to talk about suffering as the door to the depth of truth ... What an insight!

Well, what are your depths – and mine? Out of what depths do we cry to the Lord? We need to ask that question imaginatively before we say the psalm. For it's there, I think, that Psalm 130 begins.

'Out of the deep have I called unto thee, O Lord: Lord, hear my voice.' It's not a phrase we can aways peacefully recite. Sometimes it has to be more a scream, like someone locked out screaming to be let in. From time to time we all scream that we're locked out of love. 'Lord, hear my voice!'

Then comes a verse in which the psalmist suggests that the spiritual abyss in which he finds himself has opened up because of some sin of which he is conscious. What he says is literally: 'If you should record strictly all the things I have done and the punishment they deserve, who could survive?' It's not unlike Hamlet saying, 'Use every man after his desert and who should 'scape whipping?' And Hamlet goes on, much as the psalmist, to say: 'Use them after your own honour and dignity – the less they deserve the more merit is in your bounty.'

'If thou, Lord, wilt be extreme to mark what is done amiss: O Lord, who may abide it? For there is mercy with thee: therefore shalt thou be feared.' That is one of the heights of the Old Testament. Not, there is awesome terrifying judgement with thee, therefore shalt thou be feared; but, there is mercy and forgiveness with thee, therefore shalt thou be feared.

Fear is, in a certain sense, OK if it's awesome response to the heights and depths of the mercy of God – fear that we might lose out on it. Fear is OK if we're afraid of the damage we might do, to ourselves and others. There is a loving aspect to fear when we look anxiously both ways when we cross the road. At the heart of this psalm is the depth of mercy, and fear is subordinate to that.

Some of you may know the story of Spurgeon, the great Baptist preacher. He used to tell of a woman who couldn't afford to pay her rent. So the minister went to see her with a gift. He knocked and there was no reply. He went the next day – still no reply. He went the next day, and the next and the next. Eventually, the old woman came trembling to the door. She eyed the minister fearfully. 'I heard the knocking,' she said, 'and I was afraid. I thought it was the man come for the rent.' Spurgeon says there are two pictures of God: the man who comes for the rent and the man who comes with a gift. And only the second is the Christian's God.

I think of that story when I read that verse, 'If thou, Lord, wilt be extreme to mark what is done amiss: O Lord, who may abide it? For there is mercy with thee – a gift – therefore shalt thou be feared.'

And then we come to a great metaphor concerning waiting upon God. 'I look for the Lord; my soul doth wait for him: in his word is my trust.' 'I look for the Lord.' The construction suggests time dragging on through the long hours of darkness. And then the first rays of dawn begin to appear, 'before the morning watch'. 'Like as the watchmen wait for the morning, so do our eyes look for thee, O Christ. Come with the dawning of the day.'

So this psalm is a psalm of hope – hope that emerges from the experience of the depths. The penultimate verse is the comforting exclamation: 'O Israel, trust in the Lord, for with the Lord there is mercy: and with him is plenteous redemption.' And then comes the last verse. It's difficult to find in all scripture two more conflicting verses than the first verse of this psalm and the last. It begins in the depths, but within the compass of only eight short verses it reaches the confident declaration: 'And he shall redeem Israel: from all their sins.'

It's God speaking of resurrection before Christ. God discovered and discoverable by all of us in our depths. But the brevity of the psalm in our prayer books can be misleading. It speaks of a waiting upon God which may in fact take much time, and not only time. I think of the young French Jewish writer, Simone Weil. She died in Kent of tuberculosis when she was only 34, in 1943. Her great book *Waiting on God* was published posthumously in 1951. She had a close friendship with the worker-priest Henri Perrin. She emphasized the spiritual value of waiting in patience for God. Waiting upon God is not only a matter of meditation but of being patient in practice, often patient with ourselves as well as with God.

I wrote a chant for this psalm at a very painful time some years ago when my patience with the church and God and myself had all but vanished. Music is a very important part of my imaginative life, just as thinking and writing is. It often helps me to let music minister the Bible to me, to feed my imagination. The chants for this psalm with which I was familiar were all dirge-like. I wanted a chant that would express, in its brief compass, the pain and the anger of the psalmist –

and me – but would also express his final faith and hope in the love of God.

Thank you for letting my chant be sung this morning. And thank you, God, for finally letting me arrive at a deeper faith and hope in your love.

Eric James

23

The Shakespeare Sermon

Holy Trinity Church, Stratford-on-Avon; 23 April 1999

I count it a great privilege to preach this year's Shakespeare Sermon, but such an invitation often leads to a kind of rivalry-within-the mind as to what should be the subject of the sermon. Several of my friends have said to me recently: 'I assume you'll be preaching on *Shakespeare in Love*.' 'No, I will not,' I have answered. Brilliant film that it was, and wonderfully imaginative, it had – in fact – very little to do with Shakespeare – only in fiction. Nevertheless, what Shakespeare believed about love would undoubtedly be a worthy subject for a Shakespeare Sermon.

It seemed to me, however, that in this particular year, that leads to the millennium, there is much to be said for a sermon on a subject that was undoubtedly of engrossing interest to Shakespeare: the subject of time, the mystery of time. If Shakespeare could prepare us to encounter, and indeed confront, the millennium, and if a sermon could somehow be the servant of that enterprise, it would surely be a worthwhile endeavour.

To prepare myself to preach on this great, but admittedly intimidating subject, I first of all familiarized myself again with all Shakespeare's references to time. I was surprised, I must admit, to discover well over a hundred of them. It is clear that Shakespeare was almost obsessed with time. Of couse, time has a variety of meanings, upon which we shall need to reflect. But before any reflection of ours, I have to say that what Shakespeare had to say made me aware how much most of us take time for granted: whereas he, for some reason, must have spent much time thinking, meditating upon it.

He asks, rhetorically, in a sonnet: 'Where, alack, shall Time's best jewel from Time's chest be hid?' And you feel he himself must have taken that jewel from its chest, and turned it over, and held it up to the light, time and time again. It was not long before I found myself asking: 'Why was it that Shakespeare was so held, so preoccupied, almost so haunted by time, especially in relation to mortality?'

Time is rarely a friend to Shakespeare. He speaks in the first lines of *Love's Labour's Lost* of 'cormorant devouring time'; and, in *Troilus and Cressida*, Ulysses says:

> Time hath, my Lord, a wallet at his back
> Wherein he puts alms for oblivion.

Only a few lines later, he says:

> Time is like a fashionable host
> That slightly shakes his parting guest by the hand.

And he reminds us:

>   Beauty, wit,
> High birth, vigour of bone, desert in service,
> Love, friendship, charity, are subject all
> To envious and calumniating Time.

What was it, I wonder, that made Shakespeare so negative about time?

> Mis-shapen Time, copesmate of ugly Night,
> Swift subtle post, carrier of grisly care,
> Eater of youth, false slave to false delight,
> Base watch of foes, sin's pack-horse, virtue's snare.
> Thou nursest all, and murderest all that are.
> O hear me, then, injurious shifting Time!

Those lines from *The Rape of Lucrece* make me press the question: what *was* it that made Shakespeare so negative about time, 'this bloody tyrant Time'? The answer may be simple: that he was being honest to his own experience.

It's difficult for us – or, at least, for some of us – in our time, with many of the assets of Western civilization to hand, to realize how far we have come in half a millennium. The very year Shakespeare was born, plague struck this town of Stratford. The burial register of the church for the latter half of 1564 records that plague carried off more than 200 of its inhabitants, about a sixth of its population. We do well to remember, this particular day, how precarious Shakespeare's birth must have been – and, indeed, his survival after birth. We might never have known Shakespeare.

Of his four sisters, only the second survived childhood. When William died, in 1616, he had seen the deaths of all his three brothers: Edmund in 1607; Gilbert in 1612; Richard only a year later. In 1596 he had buried his only son, Hamnet, aged eleven and a half. Add to the deaths of family the deaths of friends – such as James Burbage, Lawrence Fletcher, William Kempe, Augustine Phillips and, in 1603, Elizabeth, Queen of England – and we must conclude that Shakespeare saw enough of death to let the lips of Brutus carry what could well have been his own conviction:

> That we shall die, we know, 'tis but the time
> And drawing days out that men stand upon.

And Hotspur says simply, but with equal conviction:

> O gentlemen: the time of life is short.

Yet it would be wrong to suggest that all the thoughts of Shakespeare on time are framed by mortality.

I would agree with Frederick Turner, who in his marvellous study of *Shakespeare and the Nature of Time*, now nearly thirty years old, asserts that time is an immensely complex notion, and then divides his study into nine major aspects. Of these, he says:

> ... the most obvious is historical, objective time, time viewed from outside it: a space on which events occur ... Time is the road along which men journey; at certain points on the road, events take place. Time, in this sense, is a means of placing happenings before or after each other, of assigning dates, priorities, and sequence to what it contains. We use clocks and calendars to measure off certain segments of time: minutes, hours, days; we accept by common consent that one minute's measure by a good clock is the same length as another. In this sense, time is essentially static: change is something that takes place within it. If a man dies, 'objective' time continues.

Time, says Turner, is also the personal experience of it: the dynamic process of change and becoming. It's the journey, not the road.

Then there's time as perceived through the natural world, with its cycles and rhythms and periods; the alternation of day and night and of the seasons. Another aspect of time is revealed when we say that time is 'ripe', and speak of right and wrong time. Yet another sense and meaning is when time is conceived as the revealer and unfolder, bringing hidden things to light. Finally, there's time as rhythm, when we speak of keeping time, and of musical time, or say: 'That was perfect timing.'

Such an analysis is undoubtedly helpful. Yet, when you begin to sort Shakepeare's utterances on time, you soon realize how his words transcend such analysis, even defy it. Where, for instance, do you put Prospero's words:

> What seest thou else
> In the dark backward and abysm of time?

Shakespeare uses and chooses his metaphors with such courage and imagination that he causes us to think afresh about time:

> But you shall shine more bright in these contents

he writes in Sonnet LV

> Than unswept stone besmeared with sluttish Time.

Earlier, I remarked that Shakespeare is almost always negative about time – but not quite always. In *The Rape of Lucrece* he has a passage that could hardly be more positive:

> Time's glory is to calm contending kings,
> To unmask falsehood and bring truth to light,
> To stamp the seal of time in aged things,
> To wake the morn and sentinel the night,
> To wrong the wronger till he render right,
>   To ruinate proud buildings with thy hours,
>   And smear with dust their glittering golden towers.

And in *Two Gentlemen of Verona* there is a single sentence that is full of optimism concerning time:

> Time is the nurser of all good.

I said when I began that there was a rivalry in my mind of subjects for this sermon, but time has won. Yet, in the end, I think one has to bring together the subjects of love and time; and that is best done through the Sonnets – as is, of course, best shown in the best-loved of all the Sonnets:

> Love's not Time's fool, though rosy lips and cheeks
> Within his bending sickle's compass come.

J. B. Leishman has written:

The facts of death and transience remained for Shakespeare, as they had done for the ancients, tragic facts, facts which he could not mitigate or transform by means of a securely held theology or philosophy, but which, nevertheless, he could confront (or could not do other than confront) with the affirmation of something eternal within himself – that self which, because of the intervention of Christianity had a 'depth dimension' (to repeat Rudolf Kassner's phrase) which the selves of the ancients lacked. . . .

I doubt whether it would be possible to produce from any medieval or Renaissance poet anything really approaching this characteristically Shakespearean topic of Love as the Defier of Time . . .

Shakespeare, the creator of Juliet's Nurse and Mistress Quickly, and Falstaff; Shakespeare, the creator of Prospero, and author of that speech declaring that 'the great globe itself' would fade 'like this insubstantial pageant' and 'leave not a rack behind'; Shakespeare, the greatest of realists, is also the most uncompromising of idealists. The poet who has mirrored this world of ours more comprehensively than any other is also, perhaps, the most unworldly; and the most clear-sighted of poets is also the most visionary.

Although no one should claim Shakespeare for their own brand of orthodoxy in religion, one thing is certain. Shakespeare did not escape regular church attendance. Thus he knew intimately and employed the Genevan Bible, and often echoed the phrases of the Book of Common Prayer. 'O God who hast prepared for them that love thee such good things as pass man's understanding' would, I think, be a phrase and a sentiment that particularly commended itself to him.

Paradoxically, Shakespeare knew all too well the limitations of language in this world-of-space-and-time. But that does not mean he did not believe in another world than this. He avers, for instance, in Sonnet LXXVII:

> Thou by thy dials shady stealth mayst know
> Time's thievish progress to eternity.

Even Shakespeare, with all his gifts with words, cannot describe eternity. Yet in *A Midsummer Night's Dream* it is surely characteristic of him that he should have chosen this fanciful dream-play through which to announce, for the first time, in overt and unmistakable fashion, the conviction that underlies every one of his supreme tragedies: that this world of sense, in which we live, is but the surface of a vaster unseen world, by which our actions are inspired or overruled or otherwise affected. Part of the tragedy of Macbeth is that he is dead to any deeply spiritual perception. He says:

> But here, upon this bank and shoal of time,
> We'd jump the life to come.

I never quite feel a sermon is complete unless it contains a personal anecdote or two, by way of illustration. Let me, therefore, begin to draw my sermon to a close with two anecdotes which, I think, may illustrate and, indeed, interpret my subject.

In 1939, at the beginning of the Second World War, when I was 14, I was sent out to work. Within a year, the Blitz began. The place where I started work was destroyed and I was transferred to a riverside wharf on the south bank of the Thames, on the very site of what is now the new Globe Theatre. I worked there for the rest of the war. Shakespeare came alive for me in those six years on Bankside. A couple of hundred yards along the river was Southwark Cathedral, the church which Shakespeare knew as St Mary Overie. I learned to play the organ there. When I looked into the organ mirror I could see the gravestone of Shakespeare's actor-brother Edmund, in the very centre of the chancel.

On 12 August 1607, Edmund's illegitimate son was buried in the cemetery of St Giles', Cripplegate. Just a few months later, Edmund himself was buried south of the river, in St Mary Overie – 'with a forenoon knell of the great bell'. It was an expensive funeral. Someone of means, someone who cared about Edmund, someone close to that church of St Mary Overie, must have arranged and paid for it. The distinguished scholar Schoenbaum concludes that it was probably Edmund's prosperous brother William. The funeral was on a day when the Thames was frozen over, and men, women and children promenaded upon it.

Often, when I looked into that organ mirror, and saw that tombstone, I thought not only of Edmund but of William. It seemed to me that here was probably the most tangible sign of Shakespeare's love that is left to us: love that did what it could for a brother – or, rather, for the remains of a brother. By then Edmund was where words fail, but not where love fails. 'Love never faileth' but, as Shakespeare says, 'bears it out even to the edge of doom.'

My second anecdote took place many years later, 30 years ago, by which time I had been ordained several years and had become a

Canon of Southwark Cathedral. I was asked to preach one morning at Christ Church, Chelsea, and had decided to take *King Lear* as my subject. I'd noticed, when I went into the pulpit, that in the pew just in front of it was an old lady, bent over, and wrapped in black. She was unrecognizable as anyone in particular. After the service, the vicar said to me, 'The old lady in front of the pulpit would like to have a word with you.' She turned out to be the 85-year-old Dame Sybil Thorndike. (Had I known that, I'd never have preached on *Lear*!) To my surprise, Dame Sybil wanted me to write an oration for her, to deliver at a service of commemoration in honour of Shakespeare, on his birthday, in Southwark Cathedral – St Mary Overie – a service much like this. She wanted me first to come and have tea with her, where she lived, at Swan Court in Chelsea, to discuss what might be appropriate to include in such an oration.

The tea, to my delight, turned into a kind of private performance of Dame Sybil's favourite passages from Shakespeare. She had a great sense of humour, and strong likes and disikes. She was aware that her audience would include young people who were still at school, as well as people of her own age. She said: 'Our first object must be to stop those at school thinking of Shakespeare simply as "set books". Somehow, we must get them to think of their problems and the problems of today, and to ask: "What did Shakespeare have to say about this problem and that?" He's bound to have said *something*, something worth saying, and would have said it beautifully.'

We went through various passages in various plays, and had done most of what we had to do, when suddenly Dame Sybil exclaimed: 'The Sonnets! We must include a Sonnet or two!' It was at that moment that her actor-husband, Sir Lewis Casson, entered the room. He looked to me as old as she, and proved to be older; over 90 and very frail. It was seeing him *with her*, the two of them so aged, that made me ask to insert Sonnet LXIV – on 'Time', which ends:

> Ruin hath taught me thus to ruminate –
> That Time will come and take my love away.
> This thought is as a death, which cannot choose
> But weep to have that which it fears to lose.

But in the cathedral, on the day, the way Dame Sybil spoke those words was quite unforgettable. Lewis, her husband, was sitting in the front row of the congregation, just below the pulpit, looking even more frail and near to death than he had when we first met. Sybil looked directly at him from the pulpit, put her script down, and said, as though she were addressing him alone:

> Time will come and take *my love* away.

– she pointed with her hand, and paused for an unbearable time –

> This thought is as a *death*, which cannot choose
> But weep to have that which it fears to lose.

Time *did* take Lewis Casson away, a few weeks after that service, and Dame Sybil seven years later, in 1976.

Sybil Thorndike was a woman of great faith. But I do not believe her faith greatly differed from what Shakespeare believed. She, too, believed the mystery of time was great; that now, in time, 'we know in part'. She, too, was no stranger to the tragic aspects of time. But the mystery of time for her – as, surely for William Shakespeare – opened on to another and greater mystery; the mystery of eternal and transcendent Love.

In the last scene of *King Lear*, Lear invites Cordelia, with him, to 'take upon's the mystery of things as if we were God's spies'. What I have invited you to do today is to emulate, by God's grace, the example of William Shakespeare and take upon's the mystery of Time – and the mystery of Love – 'as if we were God's spies'.

24

The 'Home Front' Service

Guildford Cathedral; 5 March 2000

'Thou sufferedst men to ride over our heads;
we went through fire and water, and thou
broughtest us out into a wealthy place.'

Psalm 66.11

When I came to prepare what I had to say at this Commemoration Service for the Home Front, I could see no way in which I could avoid speaking very personally about my own memories of the Second World War. But I shall do so in the hope that my memories will sometimes coincide with yours, and will also stimulate you to recall memories of your own that will stir you – as mine do me – to thanksgiving, and to prayer for others, particularly those we love but see no longer and whose memory today we revere.

My first thoughts of the Second World War arose, I think, one Saturday afternoon in March 1936. I was then an 11-year-old schoolboy. My father was twiddling the knob of our wireless set, when suddenly he got what we then called a 'foreigner', and the sound of German troops marching on the cobbles of the Rhineland, and singing triumphantly as they marched in to re-occupy it. To my mother, with her memories of the First World War, it was a frightening sound, and she said to my father, with anxiety in her voice: 'Is it war?' My father said: 'No, of course not!' rather too dismissively. And I caught my mother's anxiety.

It was two years later when our home was again full of the anxiety of war: September 1938. Chamberlain had just returned to London from Munich, and at Heston airport waved his piece of paper and said: 'It is peace for our time,' and quoted Hotspur's words from Shakespeare's *Henry IV*: 'Out of this nettle, danger, I pluck this flower, safety.' Everyone was relieved, for a day or so; but then the preparation for war began.

It was about then that our vicar in my home parish opened his house to two refugees from Nazi persecution. Hans Kisch, a boy of my own age, with Jewish parents, arrived, alone, from Austria. Hans had only two suitcases with him. One was full of silk ties from his father's silk tie shop in the Piccadilly of Vienna. Hans, a lonely boy, separated from his parents, became my closest friend. The other refugee was a German pastor, Heinz Helmut Arnold. He had been imprisoned in a concentration camp. His hands had been frost-bitten as he was forced to labour in the quarry near the camp. He was prematurely aged, through his sufferings, and was a gentle reminder to us of the evils of the Nazi regime.

Stanley Baldwin had told the House of Commons in 1931: 'The bomber will always get through,' and the bombing of Barcelona in the Spanish Civil War had reinforced that belief. In 1938, Herbert Morrison appealed for volunteers to join the Auxiliary Fire Service, and able-bodied men began to help the soldiers to dig trenches in parks and other open spaces.

It was generally assumed that as soon as the war began there would be massive air raids with, not least, poison gas. I can myself remember singing:

> Underneath the spreading chestnut tree
> Neville Chamberlain said to me
> If you want to get your gas mask free
> Join the blinking ARP.

Soon, evacuation began, not only of schoolchildren but of hospitals, and most of us in London and the suburbs started erecting our own Anderson shelters. I helped my father dig ours in our back garden.

Everyone old enough will have their own memory of the first Sunday of the war. The organist of our church was a schoolmaster, and was evacuated. I was not evacuated so, at 14, as a budding organist, I played the organ for the first time for a service that morning. At 11.30 a.m., half an hour after the service had begun and half an hour after Neville Chamberlain had told the nation we were at war, the siren sounded. An air raid warden rushed into the church and told us all to 'take cover'. But where? Mercifully, the All Clear soon sounded.

Of course, by that time we had all blacked out every window in our homes, and were already familiar with the air raid warden's cry: 'Put out that light!' And by that time most people had thought how they could 'do their bit'. And by that time barrage balloons were flying above us and there were anti-aircraft sites in most of the parks. Then began what we called the 'phoney war'. The devastating air raids had not yet materialized. And there was still time to 'Dig for Victory'. A rash of allotments appeared everywhere. Food rationing began, and petrol rationing, and clothes rationing.

As a 14-year-old, I went out to work, at a riverside wharf on the Thames. There was a huge emergency water supply tank just outside our wharf, and posted on it was the most inappropriate poster there ever could be. It said: 'Herbert Morrison says: Fall In – the Firebomb Fighters'! And fire-watching soon began, at every factory and business house. Every street was asked to organize a rota, which often created problems as to where your first responsibility lay; with your home and family, or your place of work. The 'phoney war' went on for months and months, indeed, for a year.

In March 1940, Myra Hess began to play at very popular lunch-hour concerts at the National Gallery. Lower down the cultural scale we were all singing 'We're going to hang out the washing on the Siegfried line'. On the radio, Arthur Askey and Richard Murdoch kept our spirits high, as did Tommy Handley's ITMA with the celebrated German agent Funf!

It was in April 1940 that Chamberlain told the world that Hitler had 'missed the bus'. Only five days later, Hitler invaded Norway and, a month later, Belgium and the Netherlands. By 22 June, France had fallen. Churchill replaced Chamberlain. And Churchill made his unforgettable speech: 'We shall fight them on the beaches ... in the fields ... in the streets. We shall never surrender.' And the Battle of Britain began.

The first bomb on London fell on 8 June 1940, but the real blitz began on Saturday 7 September at about four in the afternoon. The sky was literally full of hundreds of German planes, and by night the London docks were a blazing furnace. The Fire Brigade called up pumps from many other regions but they were soon overwhelmed. Yet among the people there was grim determination and courage, but also humour.

Fifteen miles of platforms and tunnels on the Underground were brought into service as shelters. Between 7 September and 13 November 1940, 27,500 tons of high explosive bombs and innumerable incendiaries were dropped. The police were magnifi-cent, and so were the ARP, the WVS, the doctors, the nurses and St John's Ambulance. No one kept the statistics of how many cups of tea were poured out. Boy Scouts often acted as messengers.

I can remember the parachute from a parachute mine drifting slowly to earth over our house, and the shower of shrapnel on our roof from anti-aircraft guns. But we all went to work as usual next morning, no matter how long the train took to get into London. Then we walked through shattered streets, stepping round roped-off craters, and over fire hoses, and round buildings still burning.

The wharf I first worked at (on the north bank of the Thames by London Bridge) was destroyed; I watched it burning. So was my father's office, where Wood Street joins Cheapside. Our wharf on the south bank of the Thames, where the Globe Theatre is now, survived; and the dockers turned up for work there, leaving their shattered Bermondsey homes behind, intent on emptying the barges and turning them round before another night's raid began.

One person stays in my mind – unforgettable, unforgotten – amid all this devastation and destruction: an aged blind sailor, who sat behind the counter in a shop five minutes from the Thames, fingering a pair of scales. He sat day after day measuring out the rations for people: butter, lard, tea, sugar, dried fruit. He sums up for me the dogged determination and endurance of people in those dark days.

One Saturday afternoon, 10 May 1941, I went with a young ordinand, who had joined up, to the Queen's Hall, by the BBC, to hear a performance of Elgar's *The Dream of Gerontius* by the Royal Choral Society and the London Philharmonic Orchestra, conducted by the then Dr Malcolm Sargent. After that memorable performance, my young friend went back to duty at the Duke of York's Headquarters in Sloane Square. I went home. I had not been home long when the siren went and, for five moonlit hours, over 300 bombers did their worst. Queen's Hall itself, the Chamber of the House of Commons and many other historic buildings and churches were destroyed.

When the blitz was over, there was a long lull, during which the iron railings around London were taken away for scrap, and much paper; and people went about their work again. In 1943 women became railway porters – in dungarees – and there were clippies on the buses. The role of women was dramatically changed by the war.

I often went on Wednesdays at lunch time to hear the Methodist preacher, Dr Donald Soper. He stood on a wall of the Tower of London to address a huge crowd. I remember Soper telling us one day of the old lady who, when he asked her how she was surviving the war, replied: 'Oh. No matter what's happening, I get down by the side of my bed to say my prayers. Then I get into bed, and say: "To 'ell with 'itler".'

After the lull came D-Day, on 6 June 1944, and then the V1 and the V2 bombs. My father said to me confidingly on 14 June 1944: 'Don't tell your mother, but that plane which came down last night was a pilot-less plane.' I rather scoffed, thinking it was another of Dad's stories. But he was right. It was the first of 2,340 flying bombs. Typically, we soon called them 'doodle bugs'. But 5,500 people were killed by them, 119 when one bomb fell on the Guards' Chapel, when the choir was singing the *Te Deum*: 'To Thee all angels cry aloud, the heavens and all the powers therein.'

And then came the V2. At 6.40 a.m. on 8 September 1944, the first exploded in Chiswick, and then a second, at Epping. And between 8 September 1944 and 27 March 1945, 1,045 rockets fell on Britain, indiscriminately; on Woolworth's at Deptford, for instance, at Christmas, killing 168 people. The last V2 fell near Orpington on 27 March 1945. The Windmill Theatre was able proudly to proclaim: 'We never closed.'

It wasn't long to VE Day – 8 May 1945. Like many others, I walked around the battle-scarred city that day, photographing its beflagged ruins with crowds of others. At night the dome and cross of St Paul's were picked out by searchlight, a silent yet eloquent and triumphant symbol of the six years of war.

'We went through fire and water, and thou broughtest us into a wealthy place.'

Then, on 6 August, on the Feast of the Transfiguration of our Lord, the atomic bomb was dropped on Hiroshima, killing at least 78,000 people; and on 9 August another was dropped on Nagasaki, killing or maiming another 100,000, and the war came to a rapid end.

At the close of his vivid and perceptive book *London at War 1939 – 1945* Philip Ziegler has an important penultimate paragraph. He writes:

> Though the structure of society may be modified, human nature is not so easily changed. The generous impulses that had sprung up under the impulses of war were to wither; the instincts of self-interest, self-

aggrandisement, self-preservation resumed their habitual sway. War soon became a memory: fearsome, horrifying, boring, depressing, sometimes glorious, sometimes even beautiful; but a memory which less and less shaped the thoughts and actions of those who had endured it. The comradeship, the courage, the self-sacrifice, were not forgotten; they were enriched by nostalgia, exalted into myth; but as guidelines for the conduct of daily life they became ever more irrelevant in a materialist world where the securing of advantage for oneself and one's family seemed the most if not invariably the all-important consideration . . .

It was that paragraph which made me look afresh at the psalm from which my text is taken. After our reflecting today on London at war, let us hear again what that psalmist had to say:

> Thou, O God, hast proved us:
> thou also hast tried us like as silver is tried.
> Thou broughtest us into the snare:
> and laidest trouble upon our loins.
> Thou sufferest men to ride over our heads:
> we went through fire and water,
> and thou broughtest us out into a wealthy place.
> I will go into thine house with burnt-offerings:
> and I will pay thee my vows,
> which I promised with my lips,
> and spake with my mouth, when I was in trouble.

The psalmist does not despise our looking back reflectively on what we have suffered. He doesn't romanticize it. He is realistic about it, not just nostalgic. And he says that even now there is time for sacrifice and fresh commitment; that any true thanksgiving which is heartfelt and not just a matter of words – and nostalgia – will end in that: sacrifice and fresh commitment. And that, I suggest, is why we are here today.

Perhaps the verse of my text is the most important of all:

> 'We went through fire and water, and thou broughtest us out into a wealthy place.'

So, *now*:

> I will go into thine house with burnt-offerings:
> and I will pay thee my vows,
> which I promised with my lips,
> and spake with my mouth, when I was in trouble.

The trouble is over. There is much for which we can and should be thankful. And there is yet time for fresh commitment and rededication to sacrifice for the common good.

25

Jesus the Prophet

All Saints, Poplar; 2 April 2000

'Jesus the prophet'. Wherever shall we start?

I'd want to start with the Jewish religion, which was – and is – a *noble* religion; but, like all religions, from time to time it needs a 'shake-up', which means it needs a 'mover and shaker'. And from time to time that's just what Israel had, in people such as Isaiah, Jeremiah, Amos, Hosea and Micah. Prophets didn't only shake up the church. They shook up the nation, because the Jewish church and the Jewish nation were in many ways one and the same.

So Jesus came in a long line of prophets. And all of them were to some extent rebels. All of them cried out for change, in the life of individuals and in the ordering of church and society. But what was *different* about Jesus as a prophet?

He certainly saw clearly the need for radical change in the life of individuals and in religion and society, and put that need in a nutshell. He announced the dawning of 'the kingdom of God', the reign of God, based on the law of love. But the first requirement of that love was justice.

With that proclamation of the kingdom, he issued a call to personal repentance; to a change of direction that would bring new life and hope, not least to the poor and marginalized in society. For the greater part of three years Jesus appears to have seen himself as God's agent in the reforming of the ancient religion of the Jews. It was to them, primarily, that he addressed his message. In the Sermon on the Mount, for instance, he says: 'Think not that I have come to abolish the Law and the Prophets. I have come not to abolish, but to fulfil them.'

Of course, there never is an appeal for radical change without someone getting very upset. And the establishment – the religious establishment, but not only the religious establishment – rejected what Jesus had to say, because they realized, rightly, that it had *revolutionary* implications. And Jesus himself, as time went on, realized that for him personally there were profound implications. Not simply profound, but fatal.

The rulers of church and state wouldn't let him get away for long with saying what he knew he had to say. He could see that the 'final sacrifice' – his death – was unavoidable. Without doubt they would want him out of the way. They would want to do away with him. Some scholars say that Jesus was a Zealot, and therefore was committed to overthrowing the Roman occupying power. In other words: Jesus, the prophet, was Jesus the radical nationalist – a kind of member of Sinn Fein. There's very little evidence for that, I think. But the rulers, Roman and Jewish, were perceptive enough to see the direction in which the Jesus Movement was going, and where it might end.

Jesus the prophet offered a new vision of God's will and purpose. His teaching had a remarkable simplicity to it. His parables of the kingdom were memorable. His stories, such as those of the Prodigal Son and the Good Samaritan, spoke to all sorts and conditions of men and women. But no one could call his message populist, that is to say, appealing to everyone without making much of a demand. At the very heart of his message was a series of tough demands as well as a promise. 'Take up your cross.' 'You have to be a peace-maker.' 'You must be pure in heart.' 'You must be merciful.' 'You have to love your enemies.' 'If you're going to be my disciple, think first. It will mean leaving a lot. Leaving a lot of your comfortable life.'

In my life I have been privileged to know some outstanding followers of Jesus the prophet. I think of Father John Groser, vicar of Christ Church, Watney Street, Wapping, when it was bombed during the war, and then of St George's-in-the-East, until he was made first Master of the Royal Foundation of St Katharine, in Butcher Row. I think of him as a prophet, not only as a parish priest, but as a Stepney Councillor.

I was privileged to spend an evening every six weeks for the last ten years of his life with Bishop Trevor Huddleston. I think I am in a position to say that *he* was a prophet, who followed Jesus the prophet. I went in his steps to where he had served: South Africa; Tanzania; Mauritius; Madagascar, the Seychelles and ... Stepney. Nelson

Mandela said of him: 'No white person has done more for South
Africa than Trevor Huddleston.' But there's little doubt that had he
not been removed from South Africa by the Superior of his
Community, the Community of the Resurrection, he would have
been imprisoned; and, since he was a diabetic, would have died there
– following Jesus the prophet.

The other day, the son of the person who helped my housekeeper
in the vicarage when I was a vicar in Camberwell, in the early 1960s,
phoned me and said: 'Oi, vicar, can you tell me who this geezer
Dietrich Bonhoeffer was?' I said, 'Why, Roy?' 'Well,' he said, 'they've
gone and put a plate on the side of my flat in Forest Hill, which gives
the dates when he lived there.'

'This geezer' – Dietrich Bonhoeffer – died in a Nazi concentration
camp, 55 years ago next Sunday. I never met him; but I met his great
friend and biographer, Eberhard Bethge (who died at 90 earlier this
week). Bonhoeffer was the minister of the German congregation in
London, at Forest Hill, from 1933 to 1934. In prison for eighteen
months before he was executed, he had some very radical and
prophetic thoughts about God, religion and the church. 'God,' he said,
'is the Beyond in the midst of life.' He said he'd come to understand
the worldliness of the Christian faith, that Jesus was certainly no
ecclesiastic, that he wasn't really a religious man in the narrow sense of
the word. He was a man living unreservedly in life's duties, problems,
successes, failures, experiences, perplexities, situations. He said he
wanted to speak of God-in-Christ 'not at the boundaries of life but at
its very centre'. His last words before his execution were sent to his
friend George Bell, then Bishop of Chichester. The message read:
'This is the end; for me the beginning of life.'

Not all the followers of Jesus the prophet I've met have been men.
I went to school in Dagenham; and that's where I got to know Janet
Lacey, who was then a youth worker with the YWCA. Later, she
became the head of Christian Aid, and started Christian Aid Week,
and raised its income from next-to-nothing to £2,000,000. In 1972,
when I was visiting Uganda, in the first year of President Amin's
ghastly regime, I went one afternoon to the Kitwe Community
Centre in the heart of the worst slums of the capital, Kampala. And
my heart lifted when I suddenly saw the foundation stone; and on it
were the words: 'This foundation stone was laid by Janet Lacey:
Director of Christian Aid', and the day and the month in 1963. Janet
walked in the steps of Jesus the prophet. Perhaps 'walked' is not quite

right, for Janet was a kind of sanctified bulldozer! You need a few of them as prophets!

I could go on with my list of people I've met who've been outstanding followers of Jesus the prophet. But I don't want to, because his message was not simply for people who would hit the headlines. His kingdom was not to be filled up with kings, not even with 'pearly kings'!

No one would have known the name Zacchaeus – that sleazy tax-collector – had Jesus not spotted him up a tree. Jesus had asked if he, Jesus, could come for a meal; so one more follower of Jesus the prophet was added to his company. But most of them were – and are – nameless.

In Lent, there's one more follower of Jesus the prophet we would do well to have in mind: Judas Iscariot. Perhaps he thought that when the prophet Jesus came to power there'd be a place for him in his 'cabinet', so to speak. I think one of the most moving passages in the whole of the New Testament is when Judas comes with a crowd, with swords and staves, and betrays Jesus to them with a kiss. What does Jesus say to his betrayer? Does he dishonour him? Does he refrain from honouring him? No. He says to him: 'Friend, wherefore art thou come?' 'Why have you come?'

The commentary on that verse, in the beautiful fourteenth-century book *Theologia Germanica* is: 'He said to Judas, when he betrayed him: "Friend, wherefore art thou come?" Just as if he had said: "Thou hatest me, and art mine enemy, yet I love thee and am thy friend." As though God, in human nature, were saying: "I am pure, simple, Goodness, and therefore I cannot wish or desire or rejoice in, or do or give anything but goodness. If I am to reward thee for thy evil and wickedness, I must do it with goodness, for I am and have nothing else."' There you have a glimpse of Jesus the prophet, and there you have the basis of our honouring not just 'good' people – whoever they may be – but *everyone*.

A last thought on 'Jesus the prophet'. Those of you who like the thrillers of Edgar Wallace will remember that the leaders of the underworld in his books were always given names like 'The Frog' or 'The Rat'. When John the Baptist introduced Jesus to the world at large – Jesus the prophet – he said: 'Behold: the Lamb!' 'Look who's coming! It's the Lamb! – the Lamb of God, who is taking away the sin of the world.' That's the difference between Jesus and other radical leaders. In him we behold the Lamb.

26

The Wisdom of Solomon?

St Mary's Abbey, West Malling; 2 July 2000

Sometimes a text – or a passage of scripture – touches one on the raw, so to speak. That was so for me with this Sunday's readings. Let me try and explain. The first reading – from the Wisdom of Solomon – says, explicitly, in 1.13: 'God did not make death.' For several reasons, I've wanted to shout out, in these last weeks: 'Well, who the hell did?!'

Of course, St Paul says: 'Since by man came death'; and that, of course, refers to Genesis, and Adam and Eve. But we know now that's not scientific or historical or, maybe, any other kind of truth.

I took down my commentary on the Wisdom of Solomon, one of the latest: 1979, by Dr David Winston, who says it was written in Greek, by a learned Jew of Alexandria, after the conquest of that city by Rome, in 30 BC, and reflects the growing infiltration of that Jewish community by Greek culture and ideas. The writer could mean – he says – that God did not make spiritual death, but the more obvious meaning is the more likely.

'What does it matter what he meant in 30 BC?' I thought. We now know that everything on earth has its terminus. We human beings have ours; so do animals; so, indeed, does the earth itself. Of course, we're more mealy-mouthed now than they were in 30 BC. We don't now always call it 'death'. We call it 'built-in obsolescence'.

But why did that verse from Wisdom anger me so much? For several reasons, all personal; but I think I should briefly share them with you.

First: a God-child of mine, Tom, threw himself under a train, outside Bath, some days ago. He was 42, born with some brain damage. He was the son of a friend of mine who was one of the greatest influences in my life, and who died from a sudden heart attack when he was 50. Tom had some writings of mine in his pocket when he died. In his wastepaper basket was found a crumpled piece of paper on which was written: 'If God is a God of love, why did he make me like I am?' Tom's funeral was ten days ago.

On the day after, a couple whom I had married came to tell me that she was five months' pregnant, but that the baby was so brain-damaged by an infection that, if and when it was born, it wouldn't even be able to turn itself over in bed. The birth of that now dead baby was induced last weekend. In one sense, God did not 'make death' for that child. The very caring and skilled doctors at King's College Hospital made it – at the request of the grieving parents.

On Tuesday of this last week, I went to the funeral of Mary, wife of Bishop Simon Phipps, a man who nearly 50 years ago altered the whole course of my life. Mary Phipps was 89 years old, and had been a psychotherapist for much of her life. She had been ill for many months, and the resources of her aged body had come to an end. After nearly 30 years of marriage, her death is a huge bereavement for Bishop Simon. But I couldn't say myself that, at 89, 'God did not make death for Mary Phipps.'

But it wasn't only the Wisdom of Solomon that raised questions for me. There was the Gospel for today, with the wonderful story of Jairus' daughter. 'My little daughter is at death's door' is one of the most poignant phrases in the New Testament. But it's no good simply saying 'God did not make death': her death. Jairus begs Jesus to come and lay hands on his daughter. But, while he is speaking, a message comes: 'Your daughter is dead.' That sentence is so final. But Jesus, in the Gospel, ignores that finality. 'She is not dead,' he says. 'She is asleep.' And they laugh at him. And he says *Talitha cumi* – which means: 'Get up, my child.' And 'immediately', the Gospel says, the child stands up and walks. I have to say: that sounds a different world from the world of Tom, dead on the railway line. Or John, his father, dropping dead from a heart attack. Or baby Alexander, so brain-damaged in the womb, when his life had hardly begun.

Frankly, I do not know what to make of that miracle of Jesus. It seems more important for me to say to myself: 'Look. You are a twenty-first-century Christian. You have to deal with twenty-first-century people, and the twenty-first-century realities of life – and death. What is the faith that you can bring to people *now,* who are in the midst of life and death, threatened by death?'

To them – and to myself – I have to say: I start and finish with God's love, revealed supremely in Christ. And I believe that God *did* make life *and* death because he is Love. And he revealed his love supremely in Christ, in his triumphant suffering and death.

One of my mother's favourite hymns was the blind Scottish preacher George Matheson's hymn: 'O Love that wilt not let me go'; that 'followest all my way', that 'seekest me through pain'. I have no doubt that love will not let Tom go – has followed him all the way – and John his father; and the baby Alexander, and the aged Mary Phipps. And you and me. I do not want to ask for Tom to be raised from the dead, like Jairus' daughter. I just want to know that God's love is there at the beginning of life, and in the middle of it, and in the end.

In the beginning, and in the end, and in the midst of life and death, the love of God is the Alpha and Omega. This life, bounded by time – that is to say, by death – is the gift of God in his love. But he has made us not simply for time but for eternity: the eternity of his love.

So we can pray to him, who in his love has prepared for us 'such good things as pass our understanding' – we can pray: 'Into thy hands of love, immortal love, we commit all whom we love but see no longer.' And here and now that faith can inform and frame our worship, as we pray 'with angels and archangels and with all the company of heaven'.

27

Matins for the Courts of Justice
Durham Cathedral; 9 July 2000

'For with the Lord there is mercy: and with
him is plenteous redemption.'
Psalm 130.7

I think I started preparing to preach to you this morning over 50 years ago, when I began preparing to be ordained. When, for instance, I began to grapple with the text of the Wisdom of Solomon, and discovered that the best translation of its very first verse was 'Love justice you who rule the earth.' That exhortation was written in Greek, by a Jew of Alexandria, after that city's conquest by Rome, 30 years before Christ.

But it was as I began regularly to recite the psalms, in training for ordination, that I was forced to reflect on the nature of God's justice. So I have chosen as my text this morning a verse from that marvellous Psalm 130, which is often known as the *De Profundis*, because of its Latin first words: 'Out of the depths have I cried unto thee, O Lord.'

The verse I have chosen from that psalm simply says: 'For with the Lord there is mercy: and with him is plenteous redemption.' But, significantly, the psalmist only says that after he has said: 'If thou, Lord, wilt be extreme to mark what is done amiss: O Lord, who may abide it?' I learnt from that psalm that the Lord in his justice may 'mark what is done amiss' – *will* mark what is done amiss. But that is not his last word; 'for with him there is mercy: and with him is plenteous redemption.' That, too, is an essential part of his justice.

The justice and mercy of God are indivisible. They are not contrary attributes. The justice of God is never complete until restoration has taken place, until the lost have been found.

God's justice can therefore be offensive to some, for it identifies with the *father* in the parable of the Prodigal, who ran out to meet his son, long before he knew of even the half-hearted sorrow the son felt for his behaviour. It identifies with Jesus' glad welcome to Zacchaeus, immersed as he was in fraudulent tax collecting. It identifies above all with Jesus' response to his executioners as they nailed him to the cross. Such is the 'gold standard' against which a Christian society must measure its treatment of those who offend, for the quality of such action is the touchstone not only of our Christian faith but of our Christian action.

It follows that resources of money and skilled care for the rehabilitation of offenders are not simply optional in a Christian society – or in a society which takes seriously the Jewish Book of Psalms, from which I take my text.

'Use every man after his desert, and who should 'scape whipping?' But God's justice – as Shakespeare perceived – is not only about desert. God's justice is about making us whole, remaking us. It's about his love: his unconquerable love, seeking and discovering the buried treasure within us all.

After I was ordained, one of my best friends was the local probation officer, who taught me much about keeping justice and redemption together in the local community.

When I left that curacy I became chaplain of Trinity College, Cambridge. There I saw a good deal of one of the Fellows, Sir Leon Radzinowicz. Raz, as he was affectionately known to us all, was an adviser to governments all over the world on crime and penal policy. He taught me that the world today is in the grip of a massive and seemingly irreversible crime wave. Yet few people were more concerned with redemption than Raz.

When I returned to London, to be vicar of St George's, Camberwell, the Trinity College Mission, Raz asked me to do all I could to help the Cambridge Institute of Criminology to establish a particular project, which was to be based on my neighbourhood and locality: a study of over 400 schoolboys, from 8 to 18 years, to see if there was any clear answer to the question: 'Who becomes delinquent?'

When you looked at the findings of that study, you could not simply fix on the delinquency of this or that person; you had to think of their situation, which had played so large a part in their delinquency, and to think of the redemption not only of the individual schoolboy, but of the redemption of the situation which had almost invariably played a significant part in their delinquency. It was a great help to me, as a parish priest, to have that study carried out – and carried out 'in my patch', so to speak.

In the course of my long ministry I have, in fact, been privileged to have had a diverse involvement with justice and mercy.

In 1983, I succeeded in persuading Robert Runcie, then Archbishop of Canterbury, to set up his Commission on Urban Priority Areas, the Report of which, *Faith in the City*, was published in 1985. One of its main sections was specifically on Order and Law. We learned much about justice in the Urban Priority Areas as we visited many of the cities of Britain, including Newcastle and Sunderland and Middlesbrough. I was privileged to be the presenter of a BBC television documentary on Middlesbrough which was shown on the eve of the launch of the Report. It was typical of the kindness we received in our work as a Commission that I was invited to sit in Court in Middlesbrough with the Presiding Judge of the North Eastern Circuit to learn at first hand of justice and mercy in this part of Britain.

Now that I'm 75, I serve on only one committee of the Church of England, and that is the one that looks after those clergy who, alas, have been inhibited from ministry through some serious offence – maybe to do with money, sex, or drink, or drugs. I carefully call them 'my fellow delinquent clergy' – for we are all delinquent. The Archbishop's Pastoral Advisers is the official name of the committee. Each of its members has pastoral responsibility for one, two, or more delinquents. Recently, we have set up a subcommittee to work on the subject of the redemption of delinquent clergy. It seemed to us that it was not only right that some clergy should be inhibited from ministry, but that the church should be an example of the redemption of those who had literally 'fallen from grace'. Some would undoubtedly have to remain permanently inhibited from practising their priesthood, but not all.

I make mention of this ecclesiastical committee, concerned entirely with the ordained ministry, simply by way of example: for, in the end, justice and mercy have primarily to be worked out in the Courts of Justice of our land.

I was therefore more encouraged to learn of the seminar, held in April of last year, at the Institute for Public Policy Research, under the auspices of a body that carefully called itself the Restorative Justice Commission. Its Report was entitled *Restorative Justice from Margins to*

Mainstream and it would, I believe, reward the attention of everyone involved in the practice of the Law at its very different levels. The concluding remarks of the chairman of the seminar are extremely relevant to my subject this morning: justice and mercy. He said:

> It seems that the role of restorative justice in relation to the criminal system was assumed by everyone to be a complementary one ... that its first large-scale application will be in the context of the Youth Justice system, and the new legislation in that respect – although it is implicit in what we are saying that it can grow outwards from there to include all offenders.
>
> The questions were raised as to what research is needed – and how best to present the benefits of restorative justice to the public (including the judiciary and other criminal justice professionals).
>
> With respect to engendering public support and enthusiasm, we seem to have agreed that criteria need to be identified that are meaningful to the public ... Among these we identified reductions in subsequent offending, victim satisfaction, reduction in the fear of crime, perceptions of fairness in the process, family participation and benefits to families – both victim's and offender's, and to the community at large ...
>
> It seems that we need to be able to involve individuals (both professional and community members) in the development of restorative justice ...
>
> I believe that the picture for restorative justice in the very near future will be that it has moved from the margins to part of the mainstream.

I began with my text from a psalm, and it may seem to some that it has got lost on the way. On the contrary, I would maintain it has been with us in everything I've said. And I am persuaded that if we believe that 'with the Lord there is mercy, and with him is plenteous redemption', we cannot escape commitment to policies of restorative justice, and commitment to bringing those policies 'from the margins to the mainstream'.

28

Guy Fawkes and the Gospel

Westminster Abbey; 5 November 2000

I'm aware that a lot of those who come here, to the evening service at Westminster Abbey, come from beyond the shores of Britain and, therefore, some may not understand the particular significance of today – 5 November – in this country. Let me then tell you that as a small boy I was taught, like almost every other small boy, a verse:

> Please to remember
> The Fifth of November,
> Gunpowder treason and plot.

So that if, on your way to the Abbey this evening, you saw some fireworks in the sky, and heard some minor explosions, the reason behind them is probably that, ever since 1605, 5 November has been celebrated in England, and known as 'Guy Fawkes' Night'. Fawkes was deputed to fire the gunpowder which had been placed in barrels, under the Houses of Parliament, and had undertaken to watch the cellar by himself, unaware that the plot had become known to the Court, two days before. A few days later, Guy Fawkes revealed, under torture, the names of his fellow conspirators. Eventually, he was tried and hanged - on 31 January 1606.

Guy Fawkes had become a Roman Catholic at an early age, and had been inspired with fanatical zeal for Roman Catholicism. He had plotted with several Roman Catholics to blow up the king, his ministers, and the members of both Houses of Parliament – the Commons and the Lords – in the hope that Roman Catholics might be enabled to seize the reins of government. Alas, it resulted only in the greater unpopularity of Roman Catholics at that time. A form of

service to commemorate the frustration of the Gunpowder Plot was
added to the Book of Common Prayer, to be used, annually, on 5
November, and was available for use from 1605 until the 1850s.

You may say, and with good reason: 'We did not come here this
evening for a history lesson. We came to hear the Gospel. Haven't
you something of the Gospel to share with us this evening?' And I
have. But I don't want entirely to separate the Gospel from the events
I have already described to you. I want to say to you, first of all, that
history – your nation's history, wherever you may come from – is part
of God's creation. And a history lesson always tells us something
about God's creation, and that is part of the Gospel.

Jesus' oft-repeated phrase 'The kingdom of heaven' also has a lot to
say about politics: about the kind of rulers we have, or should have,
and the kind of government; and about the way we appoint our rulers
– and, indeed, how we should get rid of them. The Gospel has a lot to
say about the roughness of human history: about the good and bad
things we human beings get up to – in our individual lives, in our
corporate lives, in our countryside, our towns, our cities, and our
nations – not just now, but in the past as well. These particular events
I've described - fanatical devotion to one of the major Christian
churches, and equally fanatical devotion against another form of the
Christian religion – the Gospel surely has something to say about that
as well.

Our modern world is a very divided world – tragically divided –
between different religions and races in, for instance, Palestine: Jew
and Arab. And still there are, alas, divisions between Christians:
Protestant and Catholic in, for instance, Northern Ireland. And here
tonight we need to confess with shame our share in those divisions.

St Paul reminds us that 'Now we know in part'; so that those who
think they have the whole truth of God *now* are – at the least – not very
'Pauline'. The Gospel should make us look for the truth of God
revealed in Christ wherever we can find it. That Gospel teaches us
much about humility before the truth. But, at this point, there is one
more bit of history that particularly concerns this Abbey, and this
evening, where and when, for one reason and another, we are, under
God, gathered together. And I want very much to set before you this
evening that piece of history, and relate it to the Gospel of Jesus Christ.

The Dean of Westminster in the early days of the seventeenth
century, at the time of the Gunpowder Plot, was a very scholarly and a
very holy man: Lancelot Andrewes. His book of private prayers is

used by many today. He was one of the chief translators of the
Authorized Version of the Bible. Much of the translation took place
in the Jerusalem Chamber of this Abbey. Andrewes was a great
preacher. He had been Dean here since 1601, and had been
consecrated Bishop of Chichester here on the very day that the
existence of the Gunpowder Plot was revealed to the King. On this
day, 5 November, he would, as a bishop, have been qualified to take
his seat in the House of Lords for the first time – 395 years ago. He
would have been there when the planned explosion was to have taken
place. So it's not surprising that Andrewes fully shared the horror of
the populace at the discovery of such iniquity.

Andrewes preached several sermons on the Gunpowder Plot, not
least on this anniversary day: 5 November. If I just tell you some of
the texts he used for those sermons, I think you'll gain an idea of what
he said; and you can picture his hearers hanging on his words:

> 'That we being delivered out of the hands of our enemies might serve
>   him without fear' (Luke 1. 74–5).
> 'Touch not mine Anointed' (I Chron. 16.22).
> 'And Cushi answered: "The enemies of my Lord the King and all that
>   rise up against thee to do thee hurt, be as that young man is"'(II
>   Sam. 18.22).
> 'By me Kings reign' (Prov. 8.15).

These weren't just narrowly 'political' sermons. His sermons revealed
Andrewes' fundamental spirituality. Let me just read you a single
paragraph of one of his Gunpowder Plot sermons:

> Glory be to Thee, O Lord, glory be to Thee; glory be to Thee, and
> glory be to Thy mercy ... the most glorious of all Thy great and high
> perfections. Glory be to Thee, and glory be to it, and to it in Thee, and
> to Thee for it; and that by all Thy works, and above them all, by us
> here; by the hearts and lungs of us all, in this place, this day, for this day,
> for the mercy of this day, for the mercy of it above all mercies, and for
> the work of this day above all the works of it. And not for this day only,
> but all the days of our life, even as long as Thy mercy endureth, and
> that 'endureth for ever' – for ever in this world, for ever in the world to
> come ... through the cistern and conduit of all Thy mercies, Jesus
> Christ.

I wanted to preach to you a topical sermon here tonight on this
5 November. And I wanted to introduce you to one of this Abbey's
greatest and most holy men. But his Gunpowder Plot sermons

cannot give you a rounded picture of the man; so I chose for the lesson this evening the story of Jesus in Gethsemane, from St Luke's Gospel. I did that because some of Andrewes' most notable sermons were preached in Holy Week and on Good Friday; and if you were to listen to those sermons – nearly 400 years old – you would certainly be brought face to face with the Gospel of our Lord Jesus Christ. So I want now to read you a short passage from a sermon Lancelot Andrewes preached before the King's Majesty at Whitehall on 6 April 1604, the Good Friday before the Gunpowder Plot.

He is preaching on a verse from the Book of Lamentations: 'Have ye no regard, O all ye that pass by the way? Consider, and behold, if ever there were sorrow like my sorrow . . .' Many paragraphs into his sermon he says:

> To be afflicted, and so afflicted as none ever was, is very much. In that affliction, to find none to respect Him or care for Him, what can be more? In all our sufferings, it is a comfort to us that nothing has befallen us, but such as others have felt the like. But here – 'if ever the like were' – that is, never the like was.
>
> Again, in our greatest pains it is a kind of ease, even to find some regard. Naturally we desire it, if we cannot be delivered, if we cannot be relieved, yet to be pitied. It sheweth there be yet some that are touched with the sense of our misery, that wish us well, and would wish us ease if they could. But this Afflicted here findeth not so much, neither the one nor the other; but is even as He were an outcast both of Heaven and earth. Now verily an heavy case, and worthy to be put in this Book of Lamentations.

Finally, I want to give you just a sentence from a sermon Andrewes preached in 1601, four years before the Gunpowder Plot. He said: 'God impeacheth not Caesar . . . in the high and heavenly work of the preservation of all our lives, persons, estates, and goods, in safety, peace and quietness, this his so great and divine benefit, he hath associated Caesar to himself.' That is, surely, an important part of the Gospel: that God has 'associated Caesar to himself'; that's to say, God has associated the work of government to himself.

What a thought that is, this week of the Presidential election in the United States! What a thought it is, this week of talks in Washington between Arab and Israeli! What a thought, with continuing talks going on this week to save the Good Friday agreement in Northern Ireland! What a thought this week, when there must be national decisions concerning the flooded areas of Great Britain. What a thought this week in Britain when important decisions on petrol and protest have to be taken – that 'God has associated Caesar to himself'.

Let us take those thoughts into our hearts and into our prayers tonight.

29

Remembrance and the Reality of War

Westminster Abbey; 12 November 2000

The word 'remember' is one of the most important in the whole of the Bible; in the Old Testament, in the Psalms, for instance: 'If I do not remember thee, let my tongue cleave to the roof of my mouth' (Ps.137.6). And in the New Testament: 'Do this in remembrance of me' (I Cor. 11.24–5). But, of course, the word 'remember' is one of the most important words there is to every human being. Yet we often assume the process of remembrance to be possible and to be important without much thought and reflection. We take it for granted.

As we entered Westminster Abbey this evening, for instance, the Unknown Warrior's tomb greeted us. But it's not only the Warrior – buried in the Abbey on 11 November 1920 – who is unknown. The whole experience of the First World War is now relatively unknown to almost all of us today. Let me remind you. The powers who lost the First World War lost 3,500,000 soldiers on the battlefield. The powers who won, the Allied Powers, the victors, lost over 5,000,000 men.

I live in Kennington, in South London, near the Imperial War Museum, and from time to time I pop in to see some of its collection of photographs and paintings of the First World War – and letters – which greatly help me to remember. And yet the reality is that there is little that can make any of us realize just what that great slaughter was like, not least for the bereaved relatives, and for the wounded of all nations who were the legacy of that war. Where remembrance is concerned, it's surprising, nevertheless, how much the poets of the First World War have done, literally, to bring *home* to people the reality of that war.

The first First World War poet to gain popularity was Rupert Brooke, whose obvious good looks appealed to people, perhaps, as much as his rather romantic words:

> If I should die, think only this of me:
>> That there's some corner of a foreign field
> That is forever England ...

Brooke died, in fact, of blood poisoning, en route for Gallipoli, on 23 April 1915, and is buried on the island of Skyros.

In 1914, Laurence Binyon, in his poem, 'For the Fallen', had penned the words that have articulated what most people have wanted to say on Remembrance Day every succeeding year:

> They shall grow not old, as we that are left grow old.

But this was still poetry that did not really confront the harshest realities of war. A more authentic poetry had to wait for poets like Siegfried Sassoon, and his poem, 'They'.

> The Bishop tells us: 'When the boys come back
> They will not be the same; for they'll have fought
> In a just cause: they lead the last attack
> On Anti-Christ; their comrades' blood has bought
> New right to breed an honourable race,
> They have challenged Death and dared him face to face.'

> 'We're none of us the same!' the boys reply.
> 'For George lost both his legs; and Bill's stone blind;
> Poor Jim's shot through the lungs and like to die;
> And Bert's gone syphilitic: you'll not find
> A chap who's served that hasn't found *some* change.'
> And the Bishop said: 'The ways of God are strange!'

Sassoon met Wilfred Owen in a hospital for the shell-shocked, and encouraged him to express his feelings in poetry. Owen had at one time considered being ordained, and had been lay assistant to a vicar, in preparation for ordination. But his experience of the war led him to an increasing revulsion at the mindless slaughter, and to question his earlier, easier beliefs. The biblical stories and the language of the Authorized Version of the Bible, which had nourished his faith, now provided him with a language for his new-found cynicism, as in his poem, 'The Parable of the Old Man and the Young', so movingly set to music in Benjamin Britten's *War Requiem*.

> Then Abram bound the youth with belts and straps,
> And builded parapets and trenches there,
> And stretchèd forth the knife to slay his son,
> When lo! an angel called him out of heaven,
> Saying, Lay not thy hand upon the lad,
> Neither do anything to him. Behold,
> A ram, caught in the thicket by his horns;
> Offer the Ram of Pride instead of him.
> But the old man would not so, but slew his son,
> And half the seed of Europe, one by one.

There was a particular army chaplain, Geoffrey Studdert-Kennedy – known as 'Woodbine Willie': a packet of Woodbines was placed on his coffin. He, like Owen, had to wrestle with how his faith could possibly relate to the horrors of the world that surrounded him. He said to a friend: 'You know, this business has made me less cocksure of much of which I was cocksure before.' In his poem 'High and Lifted Up', which he wrote as verse, to be understood by the ordinary soldiers around him, Studdert-Kennedy began with Isaiah's vision of the glory of God in the Temple. But then he says:

> God! I hate this splendid vision
> All its splendour is a lie

And he goes on:

> God, the God I love and worship, reigns in sorrow on the Tree,
> Broken, bleeding, but unconquered, very God of God to me.
> All that showy pomp of splendour, all that sheen of angel wings,
> Was but borrowed from the baubles that surround our earthly kings.
> Thought is weak and speech is weaker, and the vision that He sees
> Strikes with dumbness any preacher, brings him humbly to his knees.
> But the word that Thou hast spoken borrows nought from kings and
>   thrones,
> Vain to rack a royal palace for the echo of Thy tones:
> In a manger, in a cottage, in an honest workman's shed,
> In the homes of humble peasants, and the simple lives they led,
> In the life of one an outcast and a vagabond on earth,
> In the common things He valued, and proclaimed of priceless worth,
> And above all in the horror of the cruel death He died,
> Thou hast bid us seek Thy glory, in a criminal crucified.
> And we find it – for Thy glory is the glory of Love's loss,
> And Thou hast no other splendour but the splendour of the Cross.

The point of my sermon this Remembrance evening is to remind you – as I remind myself – that true remembrance is very costly. If you truly remember the First World War, let alone the Second, it may do to your faith what it did to some of those poets I have quoted. We all desperately need to have a faith that is able to face what those who endured the First World War had to face.

But, before I end, I want to speak briefly about another poet of the First World War whom I have only come across this year.

Charles Hamilton Sorley is probably the last of the First World War poets not to have received recognition, though an increasing number of perceptive writers have acknowledged his gifts and praised his work. He joined up at the first opportunity and was killed in October 1915. He had been educated at Marlborough College. He was the elder son of Professor William and Janetta Sorley. They were a family proud of their Scottish descent. The family had left Scotland for Cambridge, where Professor Sorley was appointed Professor of Moral Philosophy.

When Charles Sorley left school at Marlborough, he went to Germany to study, from January to August 1914. He learned the German language and made many close friends there. But then he had suddenly to return to England because of the threat of war. He was angry at his situation, that his friends in Germany must now become his enemies. He wrote: 'I am full of mute rage and arrogance and sulkiness about it.' But he joined up. When, in 1915, Sorley's kit-bag was sent home to his grieving parents, after his death, they found in it this poem:

> When you see millions of the mouthless dead
> Across your dreams in pale battalions go,
> Say not soft things as other men have said,
> That you'll remember. For you need not so.
> Give them not praise. For, deaf, how should they know
> It is not curses heaped on each gashed head?
> Nor tears. Their blind eyes see not your tears flow.
> Nor honour. It is easy to be dead.
> Say only this, 'They are dead.' Then add thereto,
> 'Yet many a better one has died before.'
> Then, scanning all the o'ercrowded mass, should you
> Perceive one face that you loved heretofore,
> It is a spook. None wears the face you knew.
> Great death has made all his for evermore.

That faith-less poem of Sorley's I read first this year. But one poem of his I came across years ago, as the words of an anthem which I learned to sing and to love. The music of the anthem was composed by Charles Wood, who was Professor of Music in Cambridge from 1924 until his death two years later. He composed the music to Charles Sorley's words in memory of his own son who had been killed in the war. At the time, most people thought that the words had been composed by Sorley during the war, since they were published in *The Times Literary Supplement* after his death, on 28 October 1915; but it later transpired they had in fact been written in Sorley's last months at school, at Marlborough. They expressed his untested schoolboy faith then; but his experience after that, at the Front, made such a faith for him, alas, a thing of the past.

The anthem – the schoolboy's words set to Charles Wood's music – Archbishop Coggan asked to be sung at his consecration as Bishop of Bradford, at his enthronement as Archbishop of York, and at his enthronement as Archbishop of Canterbury.

I read the words to you now, as we try to remember the events which so tested the faith of Sorley and of so many, with this question. Knowing now what went on then, can I voice a faith that can be expressed in such words – a faith of Sorley's which did not survive the war?

Sorley wrote:

> This sanctuary of my soul
> Unwitting I keep white and whole,
> Unlatched and lit, if Thou shoulds't care
> To enter or to tarry here.
>
> With parted lips and outstretched hands
> And listening ears thy servant stands,
> Call thou early, call thou late,
> To thy great service dedicate.

Can we still say that, after truly remembering the First World War, and the Second, and Hiroshima and Nagasaki and Vietnam and all 'man's inhumanity to man'? Studdert-Kennedy went through as much of the horror of the war as any, yet he kept his faith.

When we remember truly – what sort of faith is ours?

30

Christian Hope

The Chapel Royal, St James's Palace; 31 December 2000

'The hope which is laid up for you in heaven, whereof ye heard before in the word of the truth of the gospel.'

Colossians 1.5

I had no doubt whatever that I should preach to you this morning – this last day of the year, and many would say, of the millennium – on the subject of hope: Christian hope. But let me, at the outset, distinguish hope from optimism.

Optimism looks on the bright side of things, whatever the circumstances. It's essentially unconcerned with reality. Bernard Shaw, in his Preface to his play *Misalliance*, wrote: 'Optimistic lies have such immense therapeutic value that a doctor who cannot tell them convincingly has mistaken his profession.' Havelock Ellis said: 'The place where optimism most flourishes is the lunatic asylum.'

But we are to think together this morning about hope: about 'the hope which is laid up for you in heaven, whereof ye heard before in the word of the truth of the Gospel'. Christian hope can never escape reality; indeed, it must confront it.

This year – at 75 years of age – I have participated, somewhat inevitably, in the funerals and memorial services of several of my friends. In their last months and years, optimism would have been of little use to them. Robert Runcie, one of my dearest friends, was well aware that his time on this earth was very limited. Optimism would have done him no good whatever – indeed, it would have done him harm. But he was an example to us all of Christian hope. Of course, I have pondered long as to how best, this particular morning, I could

set before you the subject of Christian hope, and I've decided, first, to
tell you a story: from life, from recent life, from real life, from my own
life – but not only mine.

Earlier this year, I buried the five-months-in-the-womb, severely
brain-damaged foetus of Alexander, the son of two young friends of
mine, Amal and Jan. As I led the small coffin into the crematorium,
the official on duty said to me, 'Ten minutes, sir.' Such are the
realities of our secular society today. Ten minutes, for the Christian
hope and the truth of the Gospel.

You will not be surprised that I knew that, whoever else I visited
this Christmas, I must visit Jan and Amal. But it wasn't only duty that
took me to them. They are my friends. I went to have supper with
them, at their home in Brixton, the Wednesday evening before
Christmas.

As soon as I arrived, Jan put on a record: a CD of the Festival of
Lessons and Carols from King's College Chapel, Cambridge,
recorded in 1958, when the choir was conducted by David Willcocks
and the organ played by the young Simon Preston. It was recorded, as
they say, 'live'. Somewhat surprisingly I've never possessed a
recording of the King's College Carol Service, and I found that
particular recording deeply moving. There was not only the mystery
of the music, there was the mystery of time. We were 'forty years on',
yet the music had the power to move me in the year 2000. And there
was the mystery of human beings. I knew personally several of the
choral clerks who sang in that service. I used to sing Evensong each
week at King's, to give the then chaplain a day off with his family.

But it was not simply the mystery of those Cambridge human
beings that was on my mind that evening. The memory of Alexander
was, of course, still powerful. And - I haven't yet told you - the first
child of Amal and Jan - Louis - is now three years old; and I'd brought
with me a book, as a Christmas present for him, which he
immediately wanted me to read to him, while the King's record
was still being played: to read it to him while, he insisted, he sat on my
lap.

Louis is an ebullient child, and had just made his debut as an angel
in his cosmopolitan multi-faith Brixton playgroup – a rather reluctant
angel, since he really wanted to be a shepherd. When asked, 'Who are
Joseph and Mary?' Louis confidently replied: 'Jesus' Mummy and
Daddy.' But when asked, 'Then who is God?' Louis had simply
replied, after some rare moments of silence: 'Don't know.' Mercifully,

Louis was quite tired, and was soon put to bed, and we had a delicious supper, with the King's Carol Service, played a second time, in the background.

At the end of the evening, before Jan put me into a taxi to take me back home he said: 'Eric, you must have this' – and thrust the CD into my hand. So there was another mystery: the mystery of human relating and friendship.

I played that recording several times in the succeeding days, as I vainly attempted to cope with Christmas cards and presents, and, listening to that record, I realized there was at least one other mystery. As the procession slowly makes its way up King's College Chapel, at the beginning of the Festival of Carols – singing, of course, 'Once in Royal David's City' – something of the quality of that uniquely lovely building is conveyed. In other words, the mystery of beauty in architecture and art.

'But what about the carols themselves?' you may ask. 'They, surely, are the point and purpose of the service and the building. And they, surely, articulate most clearly the Christian hope.' Yes. That's true. But before we look at what the carols themselves may have to say, there is just one other aspect of that story – of the death of Alexander – that I think I need to tell you.

I went to visit Amal and Jan one Sunday morning in July in King's College Hospital, just after the dead body of Alexander had been delivered. When I arrived, Amal was cradling his body and, after a while, she asked me to do the same. As I sat with the lifeless body on my lap, I said some prayers: for Amal and Jan and Alexander. I can't remember precisely what prayers I used, but in that hospital, at that moment, I was as conscious as I have ever been of the mystery of life and death: the mystery of life ... and the mystery of death.

But, in that hospital, I was conscious also of another mystery: the mystery of compassion. Compassion makes doctors and nurses – such as those who had attended and looked after Alexander and Amal and Jan with such care and skill – give up their lives, day after day, to the task of looking after the sick and needy. The mystery of compassion is another mystery of our human nature and destiny. Where does compassion come from if not from God?

It is, I think, only when the seedbed of our soul, so to speak, has been prepared – by musing on the mystery of music; the mystery of time; the mystery of individual human beings; the mystery of friendship; the mystery of beauty in art and architecture; the mystery of life itself and the mystery of death; and the mystery of compassion – that we are ready to hear the truth of the Gospel and are able to receive the 'hope which is laid up for us in heaven'. Then we begin to understand the loving purposes of God. When we have reflected on the mystery of our own nature we can perhaps begin to understand the nature of God himself. We are open to receiving 'the truth sent from above, the truth of God, the God of love', and to learning afresh what it means that:

> He came down to earth from heaven,
>   Who is God and Lord of all,
> And his shelter was a stable,
>   And his cradle was a stall.

Of course, there's a great deal of myth surrounding the Christmas story; but let's not make the mistake of thinking that myth is always the enemy of truth. Music, I believe, is itself a kind of myth: another language for confronting ultimate reality. And, for some of us, the story, the myth of the incarnation is what one great theologian has called the 'justification of God'. Only a God who became one of us, who came alongside us, could be forgiven for all the suffering of the world; the suffering that comes not least from the gift of our freedom and from its abuse.

It's worth saying, I think, that there are at the moment, in the theological faculties of our universities, a surprising number of young people who are reading theology: not because they feel called to be ordained, not because they are 'paid up members' of the Christian church, but simply because they want to take seriously the questions that surround the mystery of their existence now and concerning, no less, the mystery of what lies ahead of all of us. And they have judged that to read theology is one of the best ways of doing just that.

I believe it's only when we take time to reflect on the manifold mysteries of our universe that we are made ready to understand him who – as the Blessing at the end of the King's College Carol Service says – 'by his incarnation gathered into one things earthly and heavenly'. And then the Christian hope in all its fullness begins to make sense, and we are renewed and made confident in the hope that

> … our eyes at last shall see him,
>   Through his own redeeming love,
> For that Child so dear and gentle
>   Is our Lord in heaven above;
> And he leads his children on
> To the place where he is gone.

His children: Robert Runcie, Alexander, all those we love but see no longer and, indeed, in time, all of us, who may share 'the hope which is laid up for us in heaven, whereof we heard before in the word of the truth of the Gospel'.

Bibliography

of books and works cited

Andrewes, Lancelot, *Preces Privatae* (Private Prayers), Methuen, 4th edn 1948 and many editions

Beausobre, Julia de, *The Woman Who Could Not Die*, Gollancz, 1948

Beveridge, Lord, *Power and Influence*, Hodder, 1953

Blake, William, *The Complete Poems*, Penguin 1977 and other editions

Brooke, Rupert, *The Collected Poems*, Sidgwick & Jackson, 1918

Dominian, Jack, *One Like Us*, Longman & Todd, 1998

Eliot, T. S., *Collected Poems* 1909–1962, Faber, 1974

Hammarskjøld, Dag, *Markings*, Faber 1964

Housman, A. E., *Collected Poems of A. E. Housman*, Cape, 1939

Huddleston, Trevor, *The True and Living God*, Collins Fontana, 1964

James, Eric, *A Life of Bishop John A.T. Robinson*, Collins, 1987

Julian of Norwich, *Revelations of Divine Love*, Penguin, 1966 and many editions

Kipling, Rudyard, *Rudyard Kipling's Verse*, Hodder, 1940

Leishman, J. B., *Themes and Variations in Shakespeare's Sonnets*, Hutchinson University Library, 1961

Macquarrie, John, *Mystery and Truth, Thinking about God* (contains the chapter 'Mystery and Truth'), SCM Press, 1975

Markov, Georgi, *The Truth that Killed*, Weidenfeld and Nicolson, 1983

Muir, Edwin, *Collected Poems, 1921–51*, Faber, 1952

Osborne, John, *Luther*, Faber, 1961

Owen, Wilfred, *Poetical Works, Collected Poems*, Chatto & Windus, 1963

Parris, Matthew, *The Great Unfrocked: Two Thousand Years of Clerical Scandals*, Robson Books, 1998

Prothero, Rowland E., *The Psalms in Human Life*, John Murray, 1903

Robinson, John A.T., *Honest to God*, SCM Press, 1963

– *The Human Face of God*, SCM Press, 1973

– *Where Three Ways Meet: Last Essays and Sermons* (contains the sermon 'Learning from Cancer'), SCM Press, 1987

Russell, George William, (A. E.), *Collected Poems*, Macmillan, 1917

Sassoon, Siegfried, *The War Poems*, Faber, 1983

Studdert-Kennedy, Geoffrey, *Poems: The Unutterable Beauty* (1947), Hodder, 1961

Teilhard de Chardin, Pierre, *Le Milieu Divin*, Collins, 1960

Tillich, Paul, *The Shaking of the Foundations*, SCM Press, 1949; Penguin, 1962

Titmuss, Richard M., *The Gift of Relationship: From Human Blood to Social Policy*, George Allen & Unwin, 1970

Turner, Frederick, *Shakespeare and the Nature of Time*, Oxford University Press, 1971

Vermes, Geza, *Providential Accidents*, SCM Press, 1998

Wallis Budge, E.A. (tr.), *The Paradise of the Fathers* (on St Anthony and the Desert Fathers), Chatto & Windus, 1907

Wavell, A. P., *Other Men's Flowers*, Cape, 1944; Penguin, 1960

Weil, Simone, *Waiting on God*, Routledge & Kegan Paul, 1951

West, Morris, *The Clowns of God*, Heinemann, 1982; Coronet 1989

Wiesel, Elie, *Night*, Penguin, 1960

Winston, David, *The Wisdom of Solomon*, Anchor Bible Commentary, Doubleday, 1970

Ziegler, Philip, *London at War 1939–1945*, Sinclair Stevenson, 1995